PYONGYANG ON THE BRINK

Pyongyang on the Brink

Sixteen Crises That Shaped North Korea

FYODOR TERTITSKIY

HURST & COMPANY, LONDON

First published in the United Kingdom in 2026 by
C. Hurst & Co. (Publishers) Ltd.,
New Wing, Somerset House, Strand, London, WC2R 1LA
© Fyodor Tertitskiy, 2026
All rights reserved.

The right of Fyodor Tertitskiy to be identified
as the author of this publication is asserted by him in accordance
with the Copyright, Designs and Patents Act, 1988.

Distributed in the United States, Canada and Latin America by
Oxford University Press,
546 Fifth Avenue, New York, NY 10036, United States of America.

A Cataloguing-in-Publication data record for this book
is available from the British Library.

ISBN: 9781805266082

EU GPSR Authorised Representative
Easy Access System Europe Oü, 16879218
Address: Mustamäe tee 50, 10621, Tallinn, Estonia
Contact Details: gpsr.requests@easproject.com, +358 40 500 3575

Printed and bound in Great Britain by Bell & Bain Ltd, Glasgow

www.hurstpublishers.com

*For Eliza Dushku,
who inspires others to inspire hope*

Contents

Acknowledgements   xi

Introduction   1

PART I
THE BIRTH OF A DIFFERENT KOREA
1940s

1. By a Single Flash   21
   America could have developed nuclear weapons earlier

2. 38th Parallel, Erased   31
   The US and the USSR could have created a unified government in Korea

3. Anyone but Kim   47
   Stalin could have selected someone other than Kim Il-sung to lead the nation

4. Murder in Pyongyang   59
   Kim Il-sung could have been killed in 1946

PART II
COLLAPSE FROM WITHIN OR WITHOUT
1950s–60s

5.	MacArthur's Triumph *North Korea could have lost the Korean War*	67
6.	The Opposition Wins *In 1956, Kim Il-sung could have been voted out of office*	79
7.	Red Giants Crush a Small Sun *Sino-Soviet political intervention could have removed Kim Il-sung from power in 1956*	91
8.	Pyongyang's Gamble, Seoul's Victory? *Kim Il-sung could have killed President Park Chung-hee and launched the Second Korean War*	101

PART III
DEATH, COUP OR WAR
1990s

9.	Shooting the Sun *Kim Il-sung and Kim Jong-il could have been killed in a 1992 coup*	113
10.	Bill Clinton's Fire and Fury *The United States could have attacked North Korea in 1993*	125

11. Crash Landing   133
   In 1994, Kim Jong-il could have boarded the medical helicopter flying to save Kim Il-sung

12. The Soldiers' Revolution   139
   The Sixth Corps' rebellion of 1995 could have succeeded

PART IV
CRACKS IN THE DYNASTY
2000s–20s

13. One-Way Train   147
   The explosion at Ryongchon Station could have claimed the life of Kim Jong-il

14. End of the Line   155
   Kim Jong-il's 2008 stroke could have proved lethal

15. Broken Bonds   161
   Unrest following the failed currency reform of 2009 could have led to a general uprising

16. The Final Stroke   171
   Kim Jong-un could have suffered a fatal heart attack in 2020

Conclusion: Future in the Past?   183

Index   189

Acknowledgements

If anyone deserves the greatest credit for setting in motion the events that made this book possible, it is Michael Dwyer, Managing Director of Hurst Publishers. Shortly after my biography of North Korea's founder, Kim Il-sung, appeared, Michael asked whether I had another book in the works. At the time I did not—but that conversation sparked the idea for the volume you now hold.

Lara Weiswelller-Wu was this book's editor, and I am grateful for her keen eye and thoughtful care of the manuscript. I would also like to express my gratitude to Daisy Leitch and Letty Allen. Without the expertise and dedication of the Hurst team, this book would never have come into being.

More than two decades have passed since Andrei Lankov's writings first drew me to Korean Studies. Since we met in 2008, Andrei has been unfailingly generous with his time and encouragement, including throughout this project.

Oliver Masheter was the manuscript's earliest reader. His precision, wit and wide knowledge of international history greatly enriched the text.

ACKNOWLEDGEMENTS

My good friend and colleague Peter Ward offered steady advice and moral support while the book was being written, for which I am deeply grateful.

Elizaveta Semyonova, my dearest friend, offered unwavering care, thoughtful perspective and invaluable advice—even lending me her laptop in a moment of urgent need.

Introduction

A Stalinist dictatorship—now there's a term that hardly feels like it belongs in the vocabulary of the modern world. It conjures up grainy black-and-white footage, military parades in Red Square and the chilling clack of typewriters signing off on midnight purges. For most readers picking up this book, it's more a ghost of history than a living reality. In fact, chances are that most of you weren't even born when, in 1956, Nikita Khrushchev stood before the 20th Congress of the Communist Party of the Soviet Union and denounced Stalinism. That moment sparked a seismic shift, triggering a domino effect across the Communist Bloc. One by one, most Communist countries began to edge away from Stalin's brutal legacy, dismantling the cults of personality and embracing, however cautiously, the path of reform.

Even the regimes that initially resisted eventually gave in to the tide of change. Today, only five nations remain under the rule of a Communist—or at least quasi-Communist—party-state. But here's the twist: four of them have radically transformed. China, Vietnam, Laos and Cuba have all, in their own ways, embraced reform. Yes, they're still one-party states, but look closer. Their citizens enjoy internet access, they can travel abroad if they choose, and their economies are booming—often outpacing those of freer societies. Social progress? In some cases, it has even leapfrogged the West. Cuba, for instance, legalised same-sex marriage before Poland, Italy or even American Samoa.

In this context, the fifth holdout—North Korea—stands out like a shadow at noon. It's not just different; it's disturbingly singular. While others turned away from the chokehold of leader worship, Pyongyang only tightened its own. Where Khrushchev shattered Stalin's image, North Korea elevated its own leaders to almost divine status—and then kept going. While China first cautiously, and then openly, allowed private enterprise to flourish, North Korea has kept its economy sealed tight, with private property remaining illegal to this day. Where countries like Yugoslavia once dared to open their borders, North Korea never followed. Only a tiny, hand-picked elite is allowed to leave, and even then, under the strictest of scrutiny. As for the internet, forget it. While the rest of the world logs on, North Koreans remain locked out. Access is granted only to a select few institutions, and something as basic as sending an email to someone outside the country can take months of bureaucratic checks and many layers of authorisation.

Indeed, few nations on Earth are as simultaneously horrifying and enduring as North Korea. It is, quite simply, one of the darkest enigmas of the modern age—a country that grips the imagination not because of what it reveals, but because of what it hides. Born out of northern Korea's occupation by the Soviets in the aftermath of Japanese defeat in 1945, this dystopian outpost of totalitarianism has defied the usual laws of history. While other autocratic regimes have crumbled under the weight of time and resistance, North Korea has somehow survived—even thrived—on repression. Eight decades on, there is no sign of softening. No glimmers of liberalisation. Just the same old iron grip, unshaken and unrelenting.

In a world where empires rise and fall, where autocracies have tumbled into democracy, where revolutions ignite and sweep away corrupt elites, North Korea remains an anomaly. A frozen relic. A monochrome state in a technicolour century, ruled not just by a dictatorship, but by a dynasty—a single bloodline clinging to power with almost mythical authority.

To live in North Korea is to surrender every part of yourself—your speech, your habits, your dreams—to the state. Surveillance is not just widespread; it is woven into the very fabric of daily life. Neighbours spy on neighbours, husbands on wives, colleagues on each other. In every home, the portraits of the ruling Kim family must hang on a designated wall, cleaned daily, worshipped regularly. Failure to care for them properly can result in execution. That is not a metaphor. That is a fact.

Every official document, every public message, every textbook must contain at least one quote from the dynastic

Leaders—not optional, but compulsory. The internet, that great equaliser of global thought, does not exist for ordinary citizens. It is a walled garden accessible only to those granted personal authorisation from Kim Jong-un himself. Imagine that: a digital world reduced to a privilege meted out by a dictator.

The punishments for stepping out of line are medieval in their cruelty. Speaking on the phone to a friend abroad, watching a South Korean drama, humming along to a forbidden pop song—these acts, banal elsewhere, can land you in one of the country's notorious labour camps. These aren't mere prisons. They are hellscapes of starvation, violence and forced toil, places where people are broken not just physically, but spiritually.

To the outside world, North Korea can feel like an eerie constant. For those who only glimpse it through headlines, and even for those of us who have spent years studying its moves, it often appears stubbornly static. Time moves forward, but inside the borders, history loops back on itself. Repression repeats. Hope flickers, then dies.

The result is a nation frozen in place—an isolated, paranoid kingdom steeped in poverty, tyranny and fear. Suffering is normalised, and truth is whatever the regime decrees. In that bleak permanence lies a warning: once a dictatorship hardens, it can endure not for years, but for generations—refusing reform, silencing its people and standing still while the rest of the world rushes ahead.

INTRODUCTION

Yet even glaciers begin as flowing water. Long before North Korea ossified into today's fortress, it was malleable, uncertain and astonishingly vulnerable. To understand how ice became iron, we must rewind to the moment when everything was still in flux.

***

Our story begins in the mid-1940s—a time of collapse, creation and enormous uncertainty. It is a truth widely observed, at least by historians, that many regimes are particularly vulnerable in their early years. Unproven, unstable and often lacking legitimacy, new states can wobble on the brink when they've barely taken form. But it is also in these tender beginnings that the deepest grooves of history are carved. The decisions made in those first frantic moments have a way of echoing across decades. So it was with North Korea.

It's easy, in hindsight, to see North Korea as inevitable—a tyrannical fixture of global politics. But there was every chance it might have turned out differently. In fact, there was even a real possibility it might never exist at all. The man who would create it—Joseph Stalin—initially had no interest in Korea whatsoever. It was only after Soviet troops swept into the northern half of the peninsula in the final days of the Second World War that Stalin began to contemplate turning Korea into a Soviet satellite. Even then, in those earliest months, he appeared open to the idea of something softer, more ambiguous. As in parts of Eastern Europe, the Soviets initially allowed a little more freedom in the North than existed in the USSR itself. Stalin even toyed with the notion of a reunified, neutral Korean state—something resembling postwar Austria, which did not fall under either the Soviet or American spheres of influence. But by mid-1946, that cautious ambiguity had faded completely. The die was cast. The Soviets were moving decisively towards the creation of a full-blown Stalinist dictatorship.

And yet, even the question of who would lead this embryonic regime was far from settled. The rise of Kim Il-sung—the man who would become North Korea's founding Great Leader, cult figurehead, and ruthless architect of one of the world's most oppressive states—was anything but preordained. When Imperial Japan surrendered, Kim was not in Korea at all. He was stranded at a remote military outpost near Khabarovsk, a lonely settlement in the Soviet Far East, serving as a junior officer in the Red Army. He was young, relatively unknown and utterly unremarkable in the grander ranks of Soviet command. It was only thanks to a curious and almost improbable chain of coincidences that his name ended up on Stalin's desk. When it did, Stalin took a gamble: Kim's next post after battalion commander would be head of state. His next rank after captain? Marshal. In one leap, Kim went from obscurity to supreme leadership.

INTRODUCTION

The early days of North Korea's existence were chaotic, uncertain and far more turbulent than you might imagine, given the later image of airtight control. Resistance to the new regime was real and, at times, organised. Borders had not yet been sealed. Surveillance had not yet calcified into omnipresence. Dissent, while dangerous, was still possible. Opposition came from factions within the North as well as from groups operating out of the South, determined to stop the consolidation of a Communist regime. The most daring of these came in 1946, when Kim Il-sung narrowly survived an assassination attempt—saved only by the quick reflexes of a nearby Soviet officer.

In these early trials, fortune played as much of a role as strategy. The crises that nearly toppled Kim before he even got started were, for the most part, random—the result of unstable conditions, rather than his own missteps. The North Korean people were not yet under total control. The political elite had not yet been purged or brought into line. But what came next would prove that, while luck had helped Kim rise, it was ruthless skill that allowed him to stay.

Once installed at the helm, Kim Il-sung proved himself an astute—and terrifying—practitioner of authoritarian rule. He learned fast and ruled hard. He grasped that power, once seized, must never be shared. And he never let it slip through his fingers again.

Kim was, in many ways, a paradox: brave and brutal, calculating yet impulsive. In the 1930s, as a young man in his twenties, he fought in the guerrilla forces of the Chinese Communist Party against Imperial Japan. This was his formative crucible—the period that shaped his worldview. There, he learned when to strike and when to retreat, when to sacrifice others for the cause, and, perhaps most crucially, when to lie. During one particularly dangerous moment, Kim—along with many others—was accused of belonging to the Group for People's Welfare, a pro-Japanese organisation that no longer existed. To survive, he had to 'confess' to something he hadn't done. He would never forget the humiliation, the injustice—and the lesson. In the Communist world, survival often required saying the unsayable, believing the unbelievable, and betraying your own truth to serve those above you.

Unlike some of his counterparts, Kim Il-sung was not a rigid ideologue. He was no Enver Hoxha—the Albanian dictator who idolised Stalin to the point of national self-destruction. Kim was far more pragmatic. He saw ideology as a tool, not a gospel.

Though introduced to Communist ideas in his school years, Kim never received a proper Marxist education. Even during his time in the Soviet military, his political training was minimal. There was a war on: Stalin needed officers who could fight, not quote Engels. As a result, Kim's grasp of Marxist theory was vague, even shallow—and that vagueness permeated his rule. North Korea would dress itself in Marxist slogans, but at its core, the regime was shaped more by power than philosophy.

That is not to say Kim always ruled wisely in his own interests. He made catastrophic errors. The boldest—and bloodiest—was also the most infamous: his decision to invade the South.

It was Kim's idea. He believed a swift strike would reunify the peninsula under his rule. He convinced Stalin to back the plan. But he had miscalculated. The United States intervened, and his regime teetered on the brink. Only the unexpected entry of Chinese forces saved North Korea from total collapse. And yet, he survived. He learned.

North Korea was born as a puppet of Moscow. While Stalin lived, Kim dared not cross him directly. But from the beginning, he was laying the groundwork to assert himself. After Stalin's death in 1953, Kim began consolidating his grip with frightening precision. Purges became his instrument of stability. Disloyal elites were weeded out, accused, imprisoned, erased. He systematically eliminated his old revolutionary comrades—just as Stalin had done before him.

Then came the ideological earthquake of 1956. Khrushchev's Secret Speech condemned Stalin's crimes and ushered in a wave of cautious reform across the Communist world. It was a direct threat to hardliners. In several countries, leaders fell. But not in Pyongyang. Kim Il-sung, ever the student of survival, responded like a master tactician. He said what needed to be said, paid lip service to the new orthodoxy, played his rivals against one another, and allowed just enough compromise to appease Moscow. And then, when the heat died down, he reversed course—regaining control inch by inch.

This was the true birth of Kim Il-sung's North Korea. A country ruled not by Marxist doctrine or Stalinist orthodoxy, but by a man who had turned power itself into an art form. And, just as he was entrenching his position, global politics handed him the perfect opportunity: the Sino-Soviet split. As Khrushchev the reformer and Mao the hardliner drifted into open hostility, Kim played both sides masterfully. He presented himself as a neutral actor, courting favour from both camps, forcing each to compete for his allegiance. And it worked. Both Moscow and Beijing bent over backwards to keep him close. Pyongyang became that rarest of beasts in the Communist world: a client state with leverage.

And thus, the system we now call North Korea took root—born of coincidence, shaped by crisis and perfected by a leader who understood that in a world of ideology, loyalty and fear could be far more powerful than belief.

***

Inside North Korea, Kim Il-sung set about building not just a state but a shrine to himself. The regime he crafted was united by a single, obsessive goal: worshipping and obeying the Great Leader. By 1967, that ambition had been formalised into doctrine. The 'Singular Thought System'—a name that gives the game away—demanded nothing less than absolute ideological obedience. No deviation. No questioning. Just total, unblinking loyalty.

This was Kim's vision in full bloom: a nation paralysed by fear, where every citizen was expected to bow, chant and praise him daily, and where the ruling elite—drawn from close friends, family and proven loyalists—functioned as a protective shell. Even better, the state was flanked by two Communist superpowers—the Soviet Union and China—both overly wary of pushing him too hard. Each one feared that if they leaned too heavily, Kim might swing toward the other. It was geopolitical blackmail, perfected.

Yet, despite the regime's apparent strength, one unhealed wound still throbbed within Kim Il-sung: the failure to conquer South Korea. That original dream, dashed by American intervention in 1950, refused to fade. And so, as the decades rolled on, the North grew ever more militarised. Consumer goods? Sacrificed for tanks and missiles. Conscription terms? Lengthened, then lengthened again. Civilians were marched into paramilitary drills. Songs glorifying the long-awaited 'final order for war' blared from loudspeakers, echoing through factories, schools and collective farms. And yet, the order never came.

Kim had learned something from that first, near-fatal gamble: never start a war you can't be sure you'll survive.

And while he came closer than most realise to launching a second invasion, he ultimately pulled back. The cost would be too high—even for him.

Instead, power, as always, prompted thoughts of posterity. Kim Il-sung had watched with disgust as the Soviet Union denounced Stalin after his death. He was determined to avoid such humiliation. Mao's decision to elevate his deputy, Lin Biao, planted a seed. What if he could choose his own successor? Someone so loyal, so personally indebted, that the dynasty could continue without challenge?

Kim's obedient, watchful firstborn son, Kim Jong-il, was the natural choice. And so, the plan was hatched. Not just to preserve power, but to pass it on, cloaked in ideology.

This was Kim Il-sung's ultimate formula for a safe dictatorship. Power above all else. Loyalty above intellect. An elite that owed everything to him. Terror to silence the people. No reforms, no concessions, no slip-ups. And, at the centre of it all, a loyal son to inherit the throne.

The cruel arithmetic worked. That's not to say that there weren't crises. Gorbachev's reforms in the late 1980s cracked open the Communist world—and with them came another brief window for change. North Korea teetered once while Kim Il-sung still lived, and again after he died in 1994, leaving behind a broken, famine-struck country for his son to rule. Yet the state survived. Luck helped. But so did the machinery of fear.

INTRODUCTION

Kim Jong-il, for his part, proved worthy of the role he had been trained for since youth. If anything, he was a less cruel man than his father. But he understood the rules of the game. A womaniser and cinephile by nature—a man who preferred directing films to directing soldiers—he knew that power did not lie in personal charisma or policy, but in maintaining the father's sacred legacy. Kim Il-sung may have died, but he had been embalmed in grandeur, preserved in a palace-mausoleum, his presence eternal. Kim Jong-il ruled as the living conduit of that legacy.

He did not reform. Even as famine swept across the land, killing hundreds of thousands—and that's a low estimate—he held the line. Aid was accepted grudgingly; too little, too late. But inside North Korea, nothing fundamental changed. Kim Jong-il's focus was survival, and for that he needed a shield. So, he did what his father had only begun: he acquired the bomb.

In 2006, North Korea successfully tested its first nuclear weapon. It was a message to the world, clear as daylight: we will not end up like Saddam Hussein. The Kims would not be toppled. Not by sanctions, not by threats, not by American firepower. The price of regime change would now be nuclear.

Still, Kim Jong-il faced his own turbulent moments. A mysterious explosion nearly killed him. An economic reform, rushed through after hardliners received his nod of approval, backfired spectacularly—triggering financial chaos and brief, flickering unrest. Some believe that, occasionally, he might have doubted himself, behind those signature dark glasses. But the doubts, if they existed, never translated into meaningful change. In the end, he followed the same logic that had kept the dynasty alive for decades: protect the system. Reject reform.

And, when his own time came, Kim Jong-il followed the family script to the letter. Like his father before him, he appointed a son, Kim Jong-un. He would leave this son little to no independent legacy of his own. Just the same mixture of economic stagnation, tight surveillance and rule by fear.

At first glance, Kim Jong-un appeared to be cut from a very different cloth. Educated in a Swiss international school, fluent in global pop culture, with a fondness for Mickey Mouse and basketball legend Dennis Rodman, he seemed more like a curious millennial than the future ruler of a 1950s-style autocracy. There were whispers of hope. Was this the moment? Was change coming?

But dynastic power has its own momentum. The legacy of Kim Il-sung—reinforced by Kim Jong-il—was too entrenched, too intoxicating to abandon. Why reform, when you can rule? Why risk anything, when you can sit upon a throne and be worshipped as a demigod?

***

In 2011, Kim Jong-un inherited a regime that was not just intact, but firmly under control. There was no serious resistance. At the time of his father's death, he held only a symbolic title—Vice-Chairman of the Central Military Commission, a ceremonial position under the Supreme Leader. But it didn't matter. No one challenged him. The elite obeyed. And Kim Jong-un did what every successful despot must: he consolidated. He purged those he mistrusted—including his own uncle and several top generals—and stepped fully into the role.

In the years that followed, he poured even more resources into the nuclear and missile programmes. Under his watch, North Korea tested long-range missiles that could, in theory, strike the continental United States. The regime had never been better armed.

From what little we know, the only genuine threat to Kim Jong-un's reign came not from generals or rebels—but from cholesterol. In 2020, rumours of a stroke swept across the internet, sparking wild speculation. Had Kim fallen into a coma? Was he dead? Was his sister taking over? The answer was 'no'. Kim re-emerged. Thinner, still very much alive—and just as resolved.

As the modern era unfolds, the outlook remains grim. The regime has succeeded in something that once seemed impossible: walling off even its vast and porous northern frontier. A towering fence now snakes along the border with China—the old escape route for tens of thousands, now blocked with steel and surveillance. The COVID-19 pandemic provided the perfect pretext for complete closure.

Before the virus struck globally in 2020, thousands of North Koreans fled every year. Afterwards, that number collapsed to double digits—and it has never recovered.

Today, escape from North Korea is not just unlikely. It is nearly unthinkable.

And while the regime may cling to mid-twentieth-century ideology, it's no Luddite. Kim Jong-un has used modern technology to enforce old-style repression. The slogans may be Stalinist, but they are now projected via PowerPoint-like presentations. Surveillance is no longer a man in a trenchcoat—it's a network of closed-circuit cameras, humming with electricity even when ordinary homes sit in darkness. When power is scarce, the state ensures the cameras stay on, even if the fridges go off.

And so the northern half of the Korean peninsula remains cloaked in darkness—literally, as satellite photos reveal, with blackout skies where the South glows brightly. But this is a nation starved not just of electricity, but of truth, safety and freedom.

To many, the story of North Korea appears to be one long, unbroken tale of despair—a place where the tyrant reigns supreme, hope is a fragile thing and the soundtrack is a mix of hush whispers, gunfire from execution grounds and choir hymns to a man with a nuclear button.

But that is not the real story.

There have been moments—sometimes thunderous, sometimes almost invisible—when North Korea has stood

INTRODUCTION

at a crossroads. Moments when history could have bent in another direction. Some of these turning points might have sparked revolution. Others could have nudged the country toward reform. A few were so subtle that, had events shifted by just a hair's breadth, even future historians might never have realised just how close the country had come to a real change.

This book explores those moments.

Inside these pages, you'll find sixteen stories—sixteen knife-edge episodes when the regime wobbled, when the future hung in the balance. My focus is on the real events: the actors involved, the forces in play and the stakes at hand. These are the flashpoints that could have transformed a nation. But at the end of each chapter, I venture briefly into speculation—a parallel track of 'what ifs'. Not wild fantasy, but grounded, historically plausible paths that North Korea might have taken, had things unfolded just a little differently during that particular crisis.

This is not just a history of what was. It's a reflection on what might have been—and why it wasn't.

Not every alternative future is a happy one. Some roads lead to new despots, cloaked in new colours, singing the same old songs. But most offer something else—a sliver of daylight, a moment of possible change. And that is the point: North Korea is not just a cautionary tale. It is a warning and a possibility.

In the end, the story of this country is double-edged. North Korea reveals what happens when one man's vanity, diplomatic cunning and hunger for absolute power are matched only by his brutal brilliance at holding on. But it also proves something else: however long the night, daylight still waits beyond the horizon. It might arrive through outside pressure, or a dictator's blunder. Or, sometimes, through the quiet, rising murmur of a people who have had enough.

Turn the page. And watch for the cracks in what was meant to be unbreakable.

PART I

THE BIRTH OF A DIFFERENT KOREA

1940s

1

By a Single Flash
America could have developed nuclear weapons earlier

February 1945. The end of the Second World War was fast approaching, and it was clear to any impartial observer that the Axis powers were on the losing side. Nearly all of France had been liberated from Nazi occupation. In the East, Soviet troops were pushing towards the Oder River. In the Pacific, American forces had reached Manila, preparing to drive the Japanese out of the Philippine capital.

It was against this backdrop that the leaders of the three Allied superpowers—Winston Churchill, Franklin D. Roosevelt and Joseph Stalin—gathered in Yalta to discuss the postwar world order. The resort city was situated in Crimea, a peninsula that had been under Nazi control only a year earlier—an impressive symbol of Allied strength.

On 4 February 1945, Roosevelt raised the topic of the Soviet Union entering the war against Japan. Stalin, recalling prior discussions with US Ambassador William Harrison, wasted no time in asking Roosevelt whether the United States was prepared to meet his demands. Stalin was looking for territorial concessions and access to vital ports in Japanese-occupied territories. Seeing Roosevelt nod in agreement, Stalin, ever the cynic, remarked, 'If the Soviet conditions are accepted, then the Soviet people would understand the USSR joining the war against Japan.'

One of the most striking features of these talks was Stalin's utter disinterest in Korea. When Roosevelt broached the subject of the peninsula, Stalin swiftly cut him off, insisting instead that they turn to the matter of securing a year-round port for the Soviet Union in the Far East. It was clear that Stalin valued such a strategic foothold far more than the fate of a peninsula home to 26 million people. Indeed, his only concern in Korea was this question of port access—he cared little about the exact location within the East, so long as it served the Soviet Union's maritime and military interests.

And so, when they finally turned to Korea, Roosevelt revived an idea the three leaders had first discussed at the Tehran Conference in 1943: placing Korea under a 'trusteeship', a sort of protectorate jointly administered by China, America and the Soviet Union. In this later session at Yalta, Churchill was not present. Roosevelt believed that this arrangement should last several decades. Stalin asked if they needed to send troops to Korea, nodding in agreement when Roosevelt assured him this would not be necessary.

The US president then probed further, asking if Stalin wanted Britain to be a co-governor of Korea. Stalin immediately acquiesced, quipping, 'If Churchill learned we weren't going to invite him, he'd kill us both.' But Roosevelt suggested involving the British only if they made a fuss about it—and Stalin readily agreed again.

The conversation left a striking impression: Stalin had no real plans for Korea and was willing to go along with whatever the Americans proposed. His speeches, publications and even restricted-access documents signed before 1945 barely mention the peninsula. Despite being Japan's largest colony, it was little more than an afterthought to a man on the verge of dominating a quarter of the planet.

The Soviet occupation of northern Korea—and the later establishment of a satellite regime—was not the result of Stalin's careful planning, then, but rather of Anglo-American strategic miscalculations. At the time, Britain and the United States believed that Soviet involvement was necessary to bring down Japan. Operation Downfall, the planned invasion of the Japanese mainland, was expected to cost hundreds of thousands of lives. The Allies had therefore agreed that the USSR would enter the war against Japan three months after Germany's surrender.

Everything changed on 16 July 1945. On that day, the United States acquired a new means to force Tokyo's surrender—the atomic bomb. The Manhattan Project, a top-secret effort to harness nuclear energy for warfare, had culminated in a successful test in the New Mexico desert. Roosevelt's successor, President Truman, wasted no time in putting this weapon to use, authorising atomic strikes on Japanese cities.

But, just as the bombings of Hiroshima and Nagasaki unfolded in early August, the Soviet Union made its move. It was no coincidence that Stalin declared war during the three days between these two attacks. Germany had capitulated on the night of 8–9 May, and, exactly three months later, Soviet troops poured into Japanese-controlled territories—bomb or no bomb.

For all the geopolitical foresight displayed by Washington, the United States was caught off-guard by the risk of a full Soviet occupation of Korea. There was no plan in place to counterbalance Moscow's influence there. With little time to react, two colonels, Dean Rusk and Charles H. Bonesteel III, were given the task of drawing up a proposal. Their resources? A *National Geographic* map of Korea—one that didn't even mark its provinces—and thirty minutes to come up with a solution.

Their decision was pragmatic: divide the peninsula along the 38th parallel. This line would create roughly equal occupation zones, making it more palatable to Stalin, while securing the key city of Keijo—now Seoul—for the United States. The proposal swiftly moved up the chain of command, gaining approval at every level—from the two colonels' superior officers to the State–War–Navy

Coordinating Committee—before landing on President Truman's desk. He signed off and sent it to Stalin.

Negotiations with the Kremlin only reinforced the impression that Stalin had little interest in Korea. He approved the proposal without hesitation and instead concentrated on trying to secure an occupation zone in Hokkaido (a request which Truman flatly denied).

And so, North and South Korea were born. Stalin's apparent indifference was further underscored by the fact that more than a month passed before he issued instructions to his forces in northern Korea, on 20 September. Tellingly, these orders contained no directive to initiate unification talks. At least to some degree, the Kremlin already saw the division as something more than a temporary measure. But could history have unfolded differently?

The plausible scenario here is an earlier Japanese surrender, preventing Soviet troops from entering Korea at all. The only way to force this outcome would have been to subject Japan to nuclear bombing before August 1945. And for that to happen, the Manhattan Project would have needed to wrap up sooner.

It is not difficult to imagine ways this might have happened. One of the key preconditions for the atomic test was procurement of uranium ore. Washington could have secured uranium supplies from Belgian Congo more quickly than it did, perhaps with assistance from its South African allies. The technical challenges of refining uranium-235—

necessary for the Hiroshima bomb—might have been resolved faster. Or the US could have obtained more raw material for a plutonium bomb, like the one dropped on Nagasaki. If even one of these processes had been accelerated, the course of history might have shifted.

There is also the question of whether Japan would have surrendered after just two nuclear attacks had the Soviet Union stayed out of the war. The records of the Japanese War Council's meetings on 9–10 August suggest that it was the Soviet declaration of war, rather than the bombings, that dominated the discussion. Foreign Minister Togo Shigenori referenced it several times, while the atomic bomb was mentioned only once, in passing, by Privy Council President Hiranuma Kiichiro. However, the sheer destruction unleashed by the bombs makes it reasonable to assume that continued nuclear strikes would soon have compelled Japanese leaders to surrender, as they came to grasp the scale of devastation and began to fear for their own lives— an atomic strike on Tokyo could have wiped out the entire Council. The archives show that it was doable: the US had already planned for further attacks after Nagasaki, with another bomb scheduled to be ready by 24 August.

Another decisive moment came when the final decision fell to Emperor Hirohito himself. His role in Imperial Japan was different from that of monarchs in Western constitutional systems. Normally, he did not govern. Even when present at Cabinet meetings, his duty was to observe in silence, lending his 'sacred presence' to the proceedings. Yet Japan, for all its authoritarian tendencies, never evolved into a personal dictatorship of the Prime Minister, either. It remained an oligarchy; and when that oligarchy was deadlocked, they turned to the emperor for his 'Sacred Decision'. When Hirohito was to speak, his word would be final.

That moment arrived on 10 August, the day after the second bomb was dropped. The War Council was split: Prime Minister Suzuki Kantaro, Foreign Minister Togo Shigenori and Navy Minister Yonai Mitsumasa were willing to accept the Allies' ultimatum for a conditional surrender, while Army Minister Anami Korechika, Chief of the Army General Staff Umezu Yoshijiro and Chief of the Navy General Staff Toyoda Soemu refused. With neither side backing down, they had no choice but to seek the emperor's ruling.

In his brief but decisive address, Hirohito made his reasoning clear. He did not dwell on the Soviet invasion. Instead, he spoke of the 'technological power' (*kikairyoku*) of the Americans and the British, signalling that Japan's leaders now understood the reality they faced. The age of nuclear warfare had begun, and with it, the world was changed forever.

Here's a plausible alternative scenario: faster progress in material gathering allows the Manhattan Project to be fast-tracked. The New Mexico test takes place weeks earlier. By the summer of 1945, Japanese cities are being systematically targeted by nuclear bombs. The War Council seeks Emperor Hirohito's decision, and he casts his decisive vote for surrender. However, his broadcast of capitulation occurs not on 15 August, as in our timeline, but earlier—just before the Soviets declare war. With Japan's surrender secured, Stalin refrains from launching his planned blitzkrieg.

The outcome would likely have been a stark contrast to what actually happened. Without the Soviet invasion, Korea, like mainland Japan, would have fallen under American occupation. In reality, the idea of a trusteeship over Korea was quickly abandoned, due to fierce opposition from the Korean elite. Even if the idea had persisted, the Soviet representative on the overseeing council would likely have found himself outvoted by his American, Chinese and possibly British counterparts. Without Soviet troops on the ground, Moscow would have had no means of enforcing its will.

Thus, in this alternative reality, it's likely that a unified, pro-American Korean state would have emerged. While it's speculative to predict its precise configuration—or even its name—it's safe to say that Seoul would probably have been its capital. This was the city's unofficial name, meaning 'capital city'; it had competed with the Japanese-imposed 'Keijo' throughout the colonial era, and with the Japanese gone, 'Seoul' would almost certainly have been recognised as the official name, as in actual history. Similarly, instead of the Soviets altering the traditional Korean flag, to the chagrin of many locals in the North, the original would likely have been hoisted across the entire peninsula.

As for the future of a united, pro-US Korea, one can only speculate. Without the Soviet invasion of Japan and Manchuria, the Chinese Communist Party would not have gained the industrial capacity of Manchuria, built by the Japanese. Without Manchuria, it's highly unlikely that the Communists would have conquered mainland China—a semi-miraculous achievement. With Chiang Kai-shek's Nationalist regime in control of China instead, a united Korean peninsula would have been less strategically significant to the US than South Korea has been for the past eight decades, as a bulwark against Communism. An undivided peninsula would have shared only a small border with the Soviet Union.

The potential consequences of this shift remain impossible to determine with certainty. Perhaps China would have stepped in instead of America? Chiang Kai-shek did have plans for postwar Korea, after all. What we can say is that the political landscape of a united Korea would have involved certain politicians from the North—including, for instance, Cho Man-shik, arguably the most notable politically active North Korean among the non-Communists—and these individuals would have reshaped Korean politics in ways that defy realistic prediction. What's more, the North's industry, built by the Japanese, would not have suffered from Communist mismanagement or war, and would have contributed to the development of the entire peninsula.

Finally, there is one person whose fate would have been drastically altered above all others': Kim Il-sung, who would never have risen to power in this alternate timeline. Most likely, he would have remained a Soviet officer in the USSR. Given his exceptional talent for political survival and his knack for manipulating his superiors, it is reasonable to assume he might have avoided Stalin's purges. In time, Kim may even have naturalised as a Soviet citizen and fulfilled what his comrades said was his ultimate dream in the 1940s—becoming a division commander in the Soviet Army.

In conclusion, two things appear clear. First, it is highly unlikely that people at the time could have grasped the immense consequences of the Soviet Union's entry into the war. Predicting the eventual division of Korea and the fall of mainland China to Communism would have been extraordinarily difficult in 1945. Even more so, the colossal human cost of the Communist regimes in China and North Korea—their longevity surpassing that of the USSR—was far from obvious at the end of the Second World War. While, undoubtedly, this alternate reality would have brought its own set of challenges and tragedies, their scale would likely have been smaller. Tens of millions of Koreans and hundreds of millions of Chinese would have lived blissfully unaware, spared the cruel fate that history has dealt them.

2

38th Parallel, Erased

The US and the USSR could have created a unified government in Korea

By the end of the Second World War, several countries found themselves split in the name of peace—and geopolitics. Germany and Austria were both carved into four occupation zones, with capitals Berlin and Vienna similarly dissected between Britain, America, the Soviet Union and, perhaps most surprisingly, France. Through the masterful diplomacy of General Charles de Gaulle, France had pulled off a remarkable rebranding: from collaborator state to victorious Allied power.

But the picture in East Asia was markedly different. After the fall of Imperial Japan, its northernmost territories—the Kuril Islands and South Sakhalin—became the Soviet Union's de facto *Lebensraum*. The native population was expelled, replaced by Soviet settlers. Japan itself was occupied by the United States. Taiwan reverted to Chinese control under the Nationalists. And then came Korea: sliced along the 38th parallel, shared between two uneasy allies—America and the Soviet Union.

As we explored in Chapter One, the 38th parallel was chosen almost on a whim—a late-night suggestion by two US colonels, rushed up the chain of command to Truman and surprisingly accepted by Stalin. At first, the division seemed a temporary arrangement. Many hoped—some even expected—that the two superpowers would hash out a deal to keep Korea united. That moment never arrived. When people later looked back, blame would be cast in every direction—South, North, Moscow, Washington, Tokyo. No one escaped accusation.

So, how did it all fall apart?

By early 1945—a landmark year in Asian history—it was clear to many that Japan's defeat was near. The country lacked the capacity to fight the United States while also battling in China and Southeast Asia.

On 14 January, the last Governor-General of Korea, Abe Nobuyuki, held a secret meeting in his palace in Keijo—now Seoul. No records were made. Attendees were allowed no notes, pens or pencils, and ordered to tell no one what was said. We only know of this meeting because a sole participant, Kayama Kaei wrote about it in 1968 (under his reclaimed Korean name, Choe Ha-yong).

The main speaker was Lieutenant-General Ihara Junjiro, Chief of Staff of the Japanese Korean Army. He delivered the news bluntly. The Imperial General Headquarters' assessment was grim. Recent reports of naval victories near Taiwan were propaganda: the real situation was dire. The navy had lost many ships, and the Empire's strength was draining fast.

Even Governor Abe was shaken. The Korean Army reported directly to Tokyo; it seemed even he hadn't grasped how bad things were. Ihara said the only hope was '*kami kaze*', the divine wind—not the kamikaze pilots, but the legendary storms that had saved Japan from Mongol invasions centuries ago. In other words, only a miracle could save the Empire.

After that meeting, Abe began preparing for the inevitable. The Allies' terms were clear—Korea was to become independent again. Abe decided they must do their best to avoid bloodshed.

Months passed, each bringing worse news. By August, after the nuclear bombings and the Soviet Union's entry into the war, defeat was not just inevitable, but imminent.

On 11 August, Abe summoned his deputy Endo Ryusaku and other officials. He asked them to speak plainly—how would the war end? After some hesitation, they admitted that defeat was near. The talk turned practical: how to prevent violence in Korea, when the end came? They agreed that Japan should bid Koreans a friendly farewell, help them build their nation, and then leave. From tomorrow, Abe announced, power would be handed to Koreans.

Urgent talks began over who these Koreans should be. Kayama suggested his friend Pak Sok-yun. Pak recommended Yo Un-hyong, a moderate independence activist on probation. Other names were proposed but refused to engage. Yo was the only one willing to negotiate.

The Imperial decree accepting surrender terms reached the Keijo headquarters at 11 p.m. on 14 August. The end was now a matter of hours. An emergency meeting was held. Endo told Nagasaki Yuzo, the official overseeing probations, that Yo Un-hyong should see him the next morning.

They met early. Endo was clear: surrender would happen that day. The Soviets were expected in Keijo by 17 August. To avoid bloodshed, the Government-General was prepared to release political prisoners and sought co-operation. Yo insisted on a hands-off approach to Korean politics. The Japanese agreed.

That day at noon, after a brief introduction and the national anthem, Japanese radio broadcast what became known as the 'Jade Voice'—Emperor Hirohito's poetic surrender speech. Delivered in classical Japanese, he solemnly accepted the Allies' terms.

The Empire listened, including those in the palace headquarters of the Government-General. When the speech ended, silence fell. Governor Abe, now carrying great responsibility, cried. He had to act fast—or blood would spill.

The ground now shifted beneath them. The very next day, independence activists set fire to Chosen-jingu—Korea's principal Shinto shrine and symbol of Japanese rule.

The Government-General feared Soviet tanks would soon roll into Keijo; but, soon, they learned the tanks would stop at the 38th parallel. With that understood, the Government-General issued a final proclamation: they remained in charge until the Americans arrived. Everyone was urged to stay calm, avoid looting and prevent violence.

In the North, the power shift was sharp and swift. On 26 August 1945, Soviet General Ivan Chistyakov accepted the surrender of local Japanese forces. Korea was split in two: the Soviet-controlled North, and a South still under Japanese rule. This was a powder keg, primed for chaos.

Lieutenant-General Kozuki Yoshio, commanding the Japanese Seventeenth Area Army (successor of the Korean Army), made a fateful move. With American forces still far away in Okinawa, Kozuki warned directly of Communist agitators and pro-independence militants plotting to disrupt peace. His tone was urgent, and the Americans listened.

Amidst the turmoil, Yo Un-hyong and his allies boldly declared the Korean People's Republic—a daring new state with ambitious claims. They announced the creation of ruling bodies: the Central People's Committee and a Cabinet, sweeping coalitions that stretched from right-wing conservatives to Communist activists. The list of members was neither discussed with the public nor with those named, some of whom rejected the idea outright. Even Syngman Rhee—the pro-American figure Yo had hoped would lead the Cabinet—refused to join.

When American troops finally landed in September, they did so cautiously. Kozuki's warnings had made an impression. After accepting the Japanese surrender, General Douglas MacArthur, the Allied occupation commander, issued a stern order. Korea would be 'free and independent'—but only 'in due course'. For now, obedience was mandatory, and acts of resistance would be punished severely.

With its Communist undertones, it's unsurprising that the Korean People's Republic was not recognised by the Americans, and quickly faded into history's shadows. But what of the Soviets?

Initially, Soviet commanders in Korea were operating without clear instructions from Moscow. In the early weeks of the postwar occupation—late August through early September—a degree of political pluralism was tolerated. Local parties, committees and activists emerged. For a fleeting moment, the future of Korea appeared to be up for debate.

That illusion faded quickly.

By 20 September, Stalin had made up his mind. Rather than co-ordinating with the Americans to establish a unified government, the Soviet leader quietly gave orders for the creation of a separate administration in the North. It was not to be overtly Communist—at least, not yet—but it was to be firmly pro-Soviet. Opposition groups were sidelined and, by October, General Chistyakov issued his own decree.

Though later framed as more democratic than MacArthur's proclamation, its essence was identical: we came to liberate you—but until you can govern yourselves, we will do it for you.

While both North and South were now under foreign military rule, one glaring absence loomed large: there was no joint organ, no shared structure, no meaningful attempt to govern Korea as a whole. The Americans, under General John R. Hodge, began appointing Koreans to subordinate roles in their military administration. The Soviets, meanwhile, waited for further instruction from Moscow—and began grooming a man the generals favoured as a potential future leader.

That man was Kim Il-sung, a former Red Army captain. On 14 October 1945, he was introduced to the Korean people as a 'national hero' in a carefully staged ceremony. His rise was then swift and symbolic. According to *Pravda*, local elections were held in the North during October and November 1945. These were the first of many votes held solely in the Soviet zone—elections that, over time, would cement the peninsula's split.

The dream of unity had not yet died—but it was slipping away. And with each missed opportunity, each unilateral decision, it became clearer: Korea's division was no accident. It was becoming policy.

It wasn't until December 1945 that the occupation parties even started to consider unification. That month, top foreign affairs officials from the Soviet Union, the United States and the British Empire met in Moscow to decide the shape of the postwar world. They agreed that Korea would fall under a 'trusteeship'—in effect, an international mandate shared between the three powers and Chiang Kai-shek's Nationalist China. The USSR and the US were to establish a joint commission to work out the details.

The moment the news reached Seoul, the South Korean political elite exploded in fury. They had believed real independence was within grasp—some were already plotting how to win upcoming elections—only to have it yanked away. The idea that Korea would once again be subjected to foreign control, however dressed up, was too much. The entire political spectrum, including even the Communists, condemned what quickly became known as the Moscow Decision.

This backlash caught the Kremlin off-guard. Moscow swiftly ordered South Korean Communists to fall in line and support the agreement. Loyal to the Party line, they U-turned, but the damage was done. American officials in Seoul took notice: watching the Communists reverse course on command, they concluded that Stalin hadn't changed one bit—and had no real intention of seeing a unified, democratic Korea.

It was in this charged and distrustful atmosphere that the unification talks finally began. The available Soviet documents show that Moscow did, at one point, consider allowing a unified government to form. The structure of this government had already been drafted by the Soviet chief delegate, Terentiy Shtykov, after consulting with Kim Il-sung and Pak Hon-yong. The prime ministership would go to Yo Un-hyong, while control over the military, police, economy and media, education, employment and foreign affairs, would all rest with pro-Soviet figures. In other words, a façade of unity masking a Communist takeover—much like what would unfold in Czechoslovakia in 1948, when Communist Prime Minister Klement Gottwald ousted the non-Communist President, Edvard Beneš.

But the proposal was never even tabled. From the first session on 20 March 1946, deadlock reigned. The Soviets insisted on rigidly adhering to the Moscow Decision—the very foundation of the Joint Commission's mandate. More controversially, they argued that only those who supported the international trusteeship should be allowed into government—conveniently narrowing it down to just the Communists. The US delegation, led by Major-General Archibald Arnold, pushed back. A Korean government, he argued, must reflect the will of the people—and if most Koreans opposed the trusteeship, then that had to be respected. Arnold also pointed out that the Soviet list of northern representatives was entirely composed of Communists and their allies. He saw no real intention from Shtykov to include democratic forces of any kind.

By May, the talks had ground to a halt. On 6 May, the Commission was suspended indefinitely. On 15 May, *Izvestiya*, the second most prominent Soviet newspaper after *Pravda*, publicly attacked the US delegation. Then in June, Syngman Rhee—the dominant figure on the South Korean right—gave voice to a new strategy: 'Although we long for a unified government, it is not achievable, so at least we must organise a provisional government or a committee in the southern region.' A month later—in a Kremlin meeting so highly classified that no internal record was kept—Stalin met Kim Il-sung and Pak Hon-yong, and gave the green light: full-scale communisation of North Korea was to begin.

Yet, in a surprising twist, the Joint Commission was revived in 1947. On paper, it seemed more serious this time around—bigger, with a network of subcommittees—but, in practice, little had changed. The handwritten notes of Soviet delegate Major-General Nikolay Lebedev, a relatively liberal figure by Soviet standards, captured the mood. Even he, writing candidly and with rare honesty (he even omitted the usual reverence when referencing Stalin), saw the Americans as barely distinguishable from fascists. The Soviets had noted the cheering crowds in the North and the cold welcome in Seoul. Their instructions were clear: revive the old plan for a joint cabinet. But there was a hitch—Yo Un-hyong, Moscow's chosen prime minister, had been assassinated by a member of the White Shirts, the same far-right group that had attempted to kill Kim Il-sung the year before. This time, the instructions simply called for a 'left-wing' candidate.

The second round of talks went just as badly as the first. Again, no unified cabinet was seriously proposed, let alone debated. By September, Major-General Lebedev had privately concluded that the process was dead. This was made official on 23 October, when the Joint Commission was dissolved and the unification issue passed to the United Nations. Both delegations left the talks convinced the other was to blame. Two Koreas were taking shape—and each believed it was the only legitimate one.

By late 1947, work was in full swing on the Constitution of the Democratic People's Republic of Korea—the North's formal name. On 11 February 1948, formerly celebrated as the founding day of Imperial Japan, a provisional constitution was unveiled, though not yet enforced. Notably, it named Seoul as the capital, denying the South's existence entirely.

In May, South Korea held elections to a Constituent Assembly. In July, the North received Moscow's green light to finalise its Constitution; the unity flag was lowered and replaced with a new one designed in the USSR. On 15 August, the southern Republic of Korea was proclaimed in Seoul, claiming sovereignty over the entire peninsula. Later that month, elections for the Supreme People's Assembly were held in the North. Astonishingly, South Korean Communists reported to Moscow that they had secretly carried out the vote in the South as well, under American noses. Shtykov, ever susceptible to wishful thinking, accepted the report at face value—even though it claimed a turnout of over 75 per cent. That three-quarters of southern Koreans would risk illegal participation in a Soviet-backed election seems laughable. But to a man convinced that every human longed to live in a Stalinist paradise, it made perfect sense.

And so, in 1948, two bitter rival states were born. Kim Il-sung and Syngman Rhee both saw themselves as the true leader of Korea—and both were ready to spill blood to prove it. But it was Kim's overlord, Stalin, who proved more willing to act. Washington remained hesitant to support the idea of marching north, wary of provoking another global war. In contrast, Stalin, emboldened by Mao's 1949 triumph in China, and convinced that the Americans would not intervene, gave Kim the green light. On the night of 25 June 1950, Soviet-supplied tanks rumbled across the 38th parallel, launching a brutal, fratricidal war that would engulf the entire peninsula.

So where had it all gone wrong? Was there a chance for a peacefully united Korea to begin with? It is tempting to conclude there wasn't one, as the goals of Stalin's Soviet Union and Truman's United States were incompatible; but a direct historical parallel shows that, even under these conditions, unification could have become a reality.

Three countries were divided by Allies by the end of the Second World War. One—Germany—remained divided for decades, before reunifying in 1990. One—Korea—remains divided to the present day, with the hope of unification slowly dying out. But one—Austria—manged to pull off a miracle and avoid the division.

The man who steered Austria back from the brink was Karl Renner—an ageing but astute Social Democrat who had already played a leading role in building the First Republic after the collapse of the Austro-Hungarian Empire in 1918. By April 1945, as Hitler's regime crumbled into ashes and Soviet troops closed in on Vienna, Renner moved swiftly. He cobbled together a coalition of politicians from Austria's pre-Anschluss (1938) parties—conservatives, socialists and Communists—to form a provisional government.

It was a bold gamble. Austria had just been part of Nazi Germany for seven years, and no one knew if the country would be reassembled or carved up like Germany. But Renner, widely seen as the father of modern Austria, managed to project the image of a united national front—broad, inclusive and, crucially, pragmatic. The Soviets, eager to claim the initiative, recognised his government almost immediately. Western hesitation followed, but by 20 October 1945, the Allies had also recognised the Renner administration as Austria's legitimate authority.

Yet the real question was whether Austria would be split. At first, it seemed inevitable. But the Communist Party fared dismally in the 1945 elections, securing little popular support. That result set off alarm bells in Moscow. Austria's economy was weak, its population small, and the idea of propping up an unpopular regime in the Soviet zone became less appealing by the day. Worse still, a divided Austria risked turning the western half into a showcase for capitalism's benefits—another West Germany in miniature.

Stalin, ever the tactician, changed course. A neutral Austria—weak, unarmed and firmly non-aligned—could serve Moscow's interests better than a drain on Soviet resources in the eastern zone and a rival state, armed to the teeth, in the western half. Stalin's moderate successors saw the wisdom too: after ten long years of occupation and negotiation, the deal was sealed.

On 15 May 1955—exactly nine years after a grim *Izvestiya* editorial signalled the death of hope for Korean unity—the Austrian State Treaty was signed. International troops pulled out. The Iron Curtain lifted. Austria stepped out of the ruins not as anyone's pawn, but as a sovereign state, treading a careful path of neutrality—and showing the world that sometimes, just sometimes, history takes an unexpected turn.

So, could Austria's miracle have been repeated in Korea? It feels like it might have been, but the changes would have needed to happen very early, and subsequent events to play out very differently.

Unlike Austria or Germany, Korea's capital was not divided. That meant the Soviets were shut out of Seoul and free to surround themselves with loyalists in Pyongyang, making them far less willing to compromise once they'd built their own Stalinist idyll there.

Ironically, Koreans had offered something like Renner's bid for a unified provisional government. The Central People's Committee of the unrecognized Korean People's Republic had been organised by a man with Japanese Governor Abe's blessing and had seemed to include figures from across the political spectrum. Yo Un-hyong himself looked like Korea's Renner—a left-wing Social Democrat with solid ties to Moscow.

But several fatal flaws had doomed the idea. First, the Americans, guarded after General Kozuki's warnings, had come to Korea thinking their job was to impose order on a rebellious populace—not to confer with grateful liberated men and women. Second, the Committee's name sounded like a Communist front rather than a genuinely politically inclusive body. Third, the proposed government lacked legitimacy even among its own would-be members—we should remember that Syngman Rhee, the slated Chairman, refused to take part. Fourth, unlike Renner, Yo had positioned himself not as leader but as second-in-command.

Still, one can imagine an alternative scenario. The plan to divide Korea is drawn up in advance of 10 August 1945. The peninsula is sliced into two to four occupation zones—perhaps with Britain and/or China joining the US and the USSR. The capital is divided too. Yo Un-hyong approaches the new authorities with a broad-church Cabinet including Communists and rightists alike. The occupiers recognise it as Korea's provisional government. In the Soviet zone there is no rival administration, and Kim Il-sung remains a deputy commandant, later returning to civilian life—maybe starting a business, as he'd once hoped. No international trusteeship is proposed, because the model for talks is clear from day one. An election is held—polls from 1945 suggest that someone like Yo would probably triumph. He forms a big-tent Cabinet and keeps it that way, balancing left and right. The USSR, still intent on securing port access above everything else, demands unfettered entry to key harbours. Once granted, Stalin agrees to withdraw. By the mid-1950s, Korea declares statehood and neutrality. And perhaps, in this timeline, a smiling Chairman Yo Un-hyong stands beside Austrian leaders at a celebratory summit—two nations, once occupied; now free, independent and whole.

Of the sixteen scenarios explored in this book, this has been one of the most often discussed—and yet was among the least likely. The miracle was possible, yes. But the stars would have had to align perfectly. The window was tiny, and once it shut, the road to division was set in stone.

3

Anyone but Kim

Stalin could have selected someone other than Kim Il-sung to lead the nation

The Soviet-Japanese War may have cracked open the Korean peninsula, yet the moment when North Korea's fate was truly sealed came not on a battlefield, but in a backroom in 1945. That was when an obscure guerrilla fighter with a murky past and a borrowed name stepped into history's spotlight: Kim Il-sung.

Barely known even among his fellow Communists, Kim—a former Manchurian insurgent and low-ranking Soviet officer—was plucked from near-anonymity and thrust into leadership by Moscow's hand. It was a gamble, and one that paid off in ways few could have imagined.

He wasn't just North Korea's first leader. He was its architect and mythmaker. It was Kim who convinced Stalin to greenlight the 1950 invasion of South Korea. Kim who, through both cunning and sheer luck, emerged unscathed from the de-Stalinisation purges that swept the Communist

Bloc later in the decade. And it was Kim who, by instituting dynastic succession, ensured that North Korea would be ruled by his family indefinitely. His imprint on the country is as profound as George Washington's on the United States—except, in this case, the nation never evolved beyond its founder's grip. With a different man in charge, North Korea might have taken a radically different path.

Who was Kim Il-sung, and why was he chosen? The son of a schoolteacher, he was born Kim Song-ju in colonial Korea in 1912. After the failure of a massive anti-colonial uprising in 1919, the family fled to neighbouring Manchuria, fearing reprisals from the Japanese regime. It was there that young Song-ju learned fluent Chinese and was introduced to Communist ideology by his schoolteacher, Shang Yue. After the Japanese army invaded Manchuria, Kim felt that this was the second home Japan had taken from him—so he joined the armed resistance, under the auspices of the Chinese Communist Party. Now actively engaged in the underground, he adopted a new name: Kim Il-sung.

The following years in Manchuria were a time of partisan struggle, marked by the hardships of life as an outcast—food shortages, purges by paranoid leadership, rare victories and a hope for triumph that grew dimmer with time. Eventually, the Japanese appointed a highly competent commander, Nozoe Masanori, to crush the resistance. Through relentless and efficient use of both carrot and stick, he succeeded. As one of the few surviving guerrilla commanders—and with a target on his back—Kim Il-sung fled to the Soviet Union.

Upon crossing the border, Kim was interrogated and settled in a secret camp in the Soviet Far East. The local military command was initially unsure what to do with him and his comrades, but the question was settled when Nazi Germany invaded the USSR in 1941. With manpower shortages mounting, the Manchurian partisans were absorbed into the Soviet Army, forming the 88th Separate Infantry Brigade—a unique unit staffed largely by foreign nationals. Kim Il-sung was commissioned as a captain and placed in command of the brigade's 1st Battalion.

During his years in the Soviet Union, Kim devoted himself to mastering Russian. Testimonies from those who knew him at the time suggest he believed he was in the USSR to stay, and learning the language seemed a prudent investment. Ironically, it proved to be just that, but for another destiny—his fluency enabled him to impress Soviet officers, ultimately propelling him to power.

By the end of the Soviet blitzkrieg, Kim Il-sung remained stationed at the 88th Brigade's base near Khabarovsk. Time was of the essence—the window to appoint new leaders for the 'liberated territories' was brief. No one understood this better than Kim's commanding officer, Zhou Baozhong. Ambitious and eager to secure a high-ranking position in Soviet-occupied Manchuria, Zhou petitioned frantically for himself and his men to be sent home. He succeeded, and orders were given. Now, fate intervened: Kim Il-sung was dispatched to Pyongyang—the very city the Soviets had chosen for their headquarters.

Indeed, Pyongyang's status as the North Korean capital was a matter of pure chance. South Korea had Seoul, which had been the nation's capital for half a millennium; but no city in the northern half of the peninsula was an obvious choice. Initially, the Soviets considered Hamhung, a port city on the Sea of Japan. The decision ultimately fell to Colonel-General Ivan Chistyakov, commander of the occupying forces. Having just returned from overseeing the Japanese garrison's surrender in Hamhung—and evidently unimpressed—he selected Pyongyang instead.

And so, the stars aligned. Upon arriving in Pyongyang, Kim's former adjutant, Mun Il, introduced him to the Soviet generals. Kim left a strong impression, and they began promoting him, while awaiting final instructions from Moscow. They even orchestrated his grand public debut on 14 October 1945, presenting him to the Korean people with much fanfare. Yet uncertainty lingered—Soviet documents from mid-December 1945 reveal that, while Kim had local support, Moscow had yet to make its final decision.

Kim Il-sung's status was finally cemented on 18 December 1945, when he was appointed Chief Secretary of the Korean Communist Party's North Korea bureau. This made him the de facto leader of the nascent state and, in that capacity, he delivered his first New Year's address to the

Korean people in early 1946. The course of history had been set.

Whom else did the Soviets consider? As of 2026, the best answer to that question comes from an unexpected place: the dry, largely forgotten minutes of an academic conference on the Korean War, held in Moscow in June 2000. Buried in those records, which were printed in the Russian town of Tula, is a presentation by Gavriil Korotkov—a Soviet military scholar who, during the Korean War, had served as an intelligence officer in the Far Eastern Military District. That position had granted him rare access to classified materials in the Soviet Defence Ministry's Central Archive.

With the Soviet Union almost ten years buried, Korotkov seemingly decided to share his findings with the world. He was careful, though. Publishing classified materials was still a criminal offence, so he avoided citing archival references, correctly assuming that, even if the authorities took an interest, the chances of tracking down the original documents were slim. The case, he probably calculated, would be dropped before it began.

Over the years, many of the sources Korotkov referenced have been declassified and verified. But one of his greatest revelations—the list of candidates considered for North Korea's top job—remains an exception.

Containing over a dozen names, this so-called 'Korotkov List' finds further corroboration in the recollections of Major-General Nikolay Lebedev, who later told his friend

Boris Krishtul that the final recommendation to Stalin came from Lavrentiy Beria, the notorious chief of the Soviet secret police. According to Lebedev, immediately after Japan's surrender in August 1945—before Kim Il-sung had even arrived in Pyongyang—the 25th Army's reconnaissance section was tasked with compiling a list of candidates based on strict criteria set by the Kremlin. But the results were unimpressive. No one met all the qualifications.

Lebedev himself reviewed the list. Unwilling to cause a conflict, he let it be sent to Moscow, where it landed on Beria's desk. Seeing that none of the candidates fit the mould, Beria recognised an opportunity to curry favour with Stalin. He ordered his agents to find a more suitable man and, once they had, he personally recommended their choice—Captain Kim Il-sung.

Lebedev's account is strikingly confirmed by another piece of evidence: Stalin's visitor logs, meticulously maintained by his guards over decades of Soviet rule. When Lebedev recounted his story to Krishtul in 1984, those records were still classified. But when they were finally unsealed, they matched his account perfectly. From 9 October to 16 December 1945, Stalin had been on holiday, leaving no entries in the visitor log. He returned to his Kremlin office on 17 December, and the final entry for that day reads: 'Comrade Beria. 21:50—23:15.' The very next day, Kim Il-sung was named Chief Secretary.

But who were Kim's rivals?

ANYONE BUT KIM

Before we go in, a few words should be said about a person who, by all logic, should have topped the list—and who, in an ultimate irony, wasn't included at all.

Pak Hon-yong, leader of the Korean Communist Party, should have been the natural pick. But history shows that, in those days, power belonged to those who were in the right place at the right time. Pak was in Seoul when Japan surrendered on 15 August, busy re-establishing the Communist Party there. By the time Soviet commanders in Pyongyang made contact with him, the shortlist had already been sent to Moscow.

This is even more striking given that, for a brief period—after the list had already been sent, but before Stalin chose Kim Il-sung—it was Pak Hon-yong who was seen as the leader of Korean Communism. In November 1945, North Korean newspapers carried slogans like 'Long live Comrade Pak Hon-yong, the leader of the Korean proletariat!' But Pak was not in Pyongyang—and that, ultimately, sealed his fate.

Now let's have a look at the list itself. Compiled in absolute secrecy, this list contained the names of individuals who did not even know they were in contention, and, to the best of our knowledge, never found out. It was a mix of ideologues, activists and Soviet loyalists: Comintern figures Kim Yong-bom, Pak Chong-ae, Chang Shi-u, Kim Gwang-jin, Pak Chong-ho and Yang Yong-sun. Then there was Kim Du-bong, a linguist and Chinese Communist Party affiliate, and Cho Man-shik, an educator and former editor of Korea's biggest newspaper, *Chosun Ilbo*. The Soviet Koreans—Aleksei Hegay, Yu Song-chol, Pak Pyong-nyul and Kim Chan—also made the cut.

Kim Il-sung's rise to power was far from inevitable. A thousand small contingencies paved his path to leadership. Had just one of these events unfolded differently, he might never have been appointed to rule North Korea: he could have been stationed somewhere other than the Soviet headquarters; Mun Il might not have taken the time to introduce him to the generals; Stalin could have picked someone from the list instead.

Perhaps the most plausible alternative scenario would have been General Chistyakov sticking to the original plan and stationing his headquarters in Hamhung rather than Pyongyang. There, another former partisan from the 88th Brigade was already stationed—Kim Chaek. A fiery man in his youth, known for aggressive opposition to the Heavenly Way—a traditional Korean religion, popular in the 1930s—he later mellowed and became known for his calm demeanour and strong organisational skills.

Kim Chaek died in 1951 during the Korean War. He left a good memory, fondly remembered in North Korea as a fair and just official, including by those who despised Kim Il-sung. He had a reputation as an intellectual—remarkable given that he had not received any formal education at all. A Soviet intelligence officer, Ivan Loboda, later regretted not having installed him as leader.

ANYONE BUT KIM

Then, of course, Stalin could have simply chosen someone from the 'Korotkov list'. Who were these people? What fate would they have brought to North Korea?

Let us have a look at those from the list on whom we know at least something beyond their official biographies.

Official documents describe Kim Yong-bom as an 'unyielding Stalinist', yet those who knew him remember a gentle man who preferred the company of children to that of politicians.

Aleksei Hegay's daughters spoke extensively about their father, and he emerges from their accounts as an ordinary bureaucrat—neither particularly kind nor especially cruel.

Some of the Soviet Koreans on the list—Yu Song-chol, Pak Pyong-nyul and Kim Chan—fled back to the USSR in the late 1950s, fearing Kim Il-sung's purges. Their post-Soviet behaviour suggests how they might have ruled. A North Korea under Yu Song-chol, for instance, might have leaned towards reform; he was open and candid with journalists about his past. Kim Chan, by contrast, would likely have been a hardliner. He rarely spoke about North Korea, believing that 'state interests' came before historical truth.

One of the most unusual names on the list was Pak Chong-ae, a woman. When the Soviet army arrived in Korea, she was languishing in prison for her Communist activities. Later, she confessed to Soviet journalists that every May Day of her time in Korea had been spent behind bars. She was physically present in the very room where North Korea was born—a Pyongyang hotel suite where Japanese commander Takeshita Yoshiharu formally surrendered to General Ivan Chistyakov. The Soviet generals were so impressed that they included her on their shortlist—an extraordinary feat, given that she was considered 'ugly' by her contemporaries. But if Pak's story was compelling enough to put her on the list, could it have swayed Stalin himself? Unlikely. The Soviet leader's misogyny was infamous.

What would have happened if someone else had been picked?

For the first few years, probably not that much. At first, the position of 'North Korean leader' was largely symbolic. The real power lay with the Soviets—their occupation administration, and later their embassy in Pyongyang.

In fact, between 1945 and 1948, Kim Il-sung was probably not even among the top five most powerful figures in North Korea. In late 1945, that position belonged to Colonel-General Ivan Chistyakov, commander of the occupying Soviet 25th Army. By early 1946, real authority had passed to Terentiy Shtykov, the Soviet Chief Representative on the Joint American-Soviet Commission on Korea. Even his deputies—Major-Generals Nikolay Lebedev and Andrei Romanenko—wielded far more influence than Kim Il-sung, who mostly rubber-stamped policies drafted by them. Even mid-ranking officers like

Colonel Aleksandr Ignatyev, who oversaw the creation of the Workers' Party of North Korea in 1946, had more practical authority than Kim.

That hierarchy persisted after North Korea's formal establishment in 1948. Soviet Ambassador Shtykov and his deputy, Tunkin, were regarded as Kim's superiors. During the Korean War, the second Soviet ambassador, Vladimir Razuvayev, held considerable sway over military decision-making. Kim Il-sung asserted more control over civilian matters, but he was still under Soviet oversight. It was only after the war, with the appointment of Ambassador Sergei Suzdalev, that Kim Il-sung could no longer be bossed around.

Any alternative leader would have faced similar constraints. The policies of the late 1940s—land reform, currency reform, the formation of the party-state—would likely have unfolded in much the same way. Even the cult would have been manufactured by the same Soviet propaganda machine—a pretty standard procedure for every new Moscow-appointed leader. Had Yang Yong-sun been chosen, he could have been hailed as the supreme leader of Korea's anti-Japanese resistance. Aleksei Hegai—who received a Korean name, Ho Ga-i—could have been recast as a great Marxist-Leninist thinker. Pak Chong-ae might have been depicted as a 'legendary revolutionary whose unbreakable spirit struck fear into the hearts of the Japanese'.

But as time passed, any North Korean leader would have gained more autonomy. Major-General Lebedev's 1940s diaries reveal that, while some Soviet officials saw their control over North Korea as permanent, others—including Lebedev himself—believed that their duty was eventually to hand over power to the Koreans. That view became dominant in Moscow after Stalin's death in 1953.

For Kim Il-sung, the first great test of his independence was the Korean War (1950–3). After much persuasion, he convinced Stalin to approve an invasion of the South. Would the war have happened under another leader? Probably not. The only other man who lobbied for war was Pak Hon-yong, who had not been considered for the top position. None of the candidates had expressed any noticeable interest in unifying Korea by force. Had the choice fallen to someone else, North Korea might have been a completely different country as early as 1950.

Instead, history turned on Kim Il-sung. One man. One decision. Decades of consequences.

4

Murder in Pyongyang
Kim Il-sung could have been killed in 1946

Kim Il-sung faced several crises that threatened his grip on power—but only one that directly and immediately threatened his life. In March 1946, he survived an assassination attempt.

By late February 1946, Kim's position as the top Korean official in the North appeared unassailable. Following his appointment as Chief Secretary in December 1945, the Soviets installed him as head of the North Korean proto-government: the Provisional People's Committee for North Korea. From the perspective of an anti-Communist Korean, it seemed all too clear that Moscow intended to extend its influence over at least the North—if not the entire peninsula—and their chosen instrument was Chairman Kim. Thus, some radical rightists concluded, the most effective form of resistance to Communism would be to eliminate him.

The group that planned the assassination called itself the White Shirts Society. Their name echoed that of their ideological patron—a quasi-fascist Chinese organisation, the Blue Shirts Society, itself a reference to the Italian Blackshirts and German Brownshirts. White, being the traditional colour of Korean dress, suited this nationalist right-wing movement perfectly.

The day the newly appointed North Korean leader was meant to die was 1 March 1946. Kim Il-sung was scheduled to address a crowd in honour of the twenty-seventh anniversary of the 1919 anti-colonial uprising. Six men were directly involved in the plot: Kim Jong-ui, the team leader; Lee Song-ryol; Kim Hyong-jip; Choe Ki-song; Lee Hui-du; and Cho Jae-guk, an official from the South Pyongan Provincial People's Committee with right-nationalist sympathies. It was Cho who supplied the group's weapons—pistols and grenades.

They arrived at the square in front of Pyongyang Station, where the speech was to take place, successfully slipping past security. The podium for the ceremony had been erected behind the station, facing the city. Each of the five conspirators took up their preplanned positions. Kim Hyong-jip stood 30 metres in front of the podium. Choe Ki-song flanked it on the left, Lee Hui-du on the right. Lee Song-ryol was positioned five metres in front of Kim Hyong-jip, while Kim Jong-ui stood 30 metres behind him. Cho Jae-guk stationed himself on the roof of the old

Pyongyang Shinmun office to capture the moment on film. The plan was simple: allow Kim Il-sung to speak for around five minutes, then have all attackers simultaneously hurl grenades at the 'national hero of the Korean people'.

As Lee Song-ryol was the closest to the podium, he was tasked with giving the signal to attack. Everything was in place. Kim Il-sung ascended the platform and addressed the crowd: 'My fellow compatriots!' And then, chaos.

Kim Hyong-jip pulled his grenade pin prematurely. Under interrogation, he later claimed to have misread the timing, was surprised that no signal had been given, and decided to act regardless. The guards spotted him, panic erupted, and Kim was forced to throw the grenade immediately. A Soviet junior lieutenant, Yakov Novichenko, sprang into action. He grabbed the grenade, but before he could hurl it away, it exploded, severing his hand. Kim Hyong-jip drew his pistol to shoot Kim Il-sung, but by then he was tackled and arrested. The North Korean leader was rushed from the scene.

Kim Hyong-jip and Kim Jong-ui, along with several others, were eventually arrested by the Soviets and executed on 12 November 1946. Kim Jong-ui was 43; Kim Hyong-jip just 18. At least one member—Cho Jae-guk—managed to escape to South Korea, where his testimony was eventually recorded and published.

This leads to a provocative question: what if the assassination had succeeded? Suppose Kim Hyong-jip had held his nerve, and the attack had gone according to plan? The assassins would almost certainly have been caught and executed—martyrs to their cause. But with Kim Il-sung dead, and in such a public, gruesome manner, the Soviets would have faced two immediate dilemmas: how to respond, and who should succeed him?

The actual attempt was swiftly buried. Neither Soviet *Pravda* nor North Korea's *Chongno* reported it. Kim Il-sung was to be portrayed as a universally beloved national hero—the suggestion that Koreans themselves had tried to kill him was ideologically intolerable. A successful assassination, however, would have made such silence impossible. *Pravda* and *Chongno* would have been obliged to publish mournful editorials proclaiming that 'Commander Kim Il-sung' had fallen to 'fascists'—an epithet not far from the truth, for a change, given the nature of the White Shirts Society. If the assassin team's links to the South were uncovered, it could have shattered what little trust remained between the Soviet administration and the United States. Indeed, as the historical record shows, by 1946 the two powers were already viewing one another with growing suspicion.

There is also the personal dimension. The Soviet chief delegate to the Joint US–USSR Commission on Korea was General Terentiy Shtykov, a man who enjoyed considerable autonomy from Moscow—and who shared a close friendship with Kim Il-sung. Both men lacked formal education: Kim was a middle school dropout; Shtykov, a vocational school graduate. They bonded deeply, often spending time together informally. When playing cards, the loser was made to crawl under the table—a silly ritual that spoke volumes about their camaraderie. Losing Kim to a terrorist attack would almost certainly have deepened Shtykov's mistrust of the Americans and hardened his stance in negotiations.

As for Kim Il-sung's potential successor, in March 1946 the most plausible candidate was Pak Hon-yong. A veteran underground revolutionary during the colonial period, Pak led the Korean Communist Party. At this time, Kim Il-sung was technically subordinate to him—the North–South party split would not occur until May. Pak had his own advocates within Soviet ranks, chiefly Anatoliy Shabshin, Vice-Consul in Seoul, and Shabshin's politically active wife, Fanya. According to those familiar with Soviet deliberations, the idea of replacing Kim with Pak would only be shelved definitively in 1949. Had Kim been assassinated, Pak would have been the obvious successor.

For a time, Pak's North Korea would have been little more than a different face on the same Soviet-controlled machine. Behind the scenes, Moscow's iron grip would have ensured that, despite the change in leadership, the country's direction remained eerily familiar—at least for a few years.

And here lies the most ironic twist in this hypothetical timeline. With unification talks collapsing, future historians might well have concluded that the failed talks were a direct result of Kim Il-sung's assassination—and blamed the assassins for the division of Korea. Moreover, Pak was one of two principal advocates for the invasion of South Korea, alongside Kim Il-sung himself. The key factor that ultimately persuaded Stalin to approve the war in 1950 was Mao's unexpected success in China the previous year—something unlikely to have been affected by Kim's death. In this alternate reality, with Pak Hon-yong as sole instigator, it would have been tempting for historians to regret Kim's death, wrongly guessing that, if only he had lived, the most destructive war in Korean history might never have happened. Thus, paradoxically, the assassination might have posthumously redeemed Kim Il-sung and led him to be remembered not as a cruel tyrant, but as a moderate alternative.

PART II

COLLAPSE FROM WITHIN OR WITHOUT

1950s-60s

5

MacArthur's Triumph
North Korea could have lost the Korean War

The most violent inferno the Korean Peninsula has ever endured was the Korean War (1950–3), a brutal clash that left over one and a half million dead and two nations shattered. And it all began with ambition.

Kim Il-sung, installed by Moscow and eager to unify the peninsula under his rule, had been itching for a fight since the late 1940s. His ally Pak Hon-yong, a South Korean Communist exiled to the North, saw war as a chance to revive his own following. As American and Soviet forces pulled out of Korea in 1948–9, the moment seemed ripe.

By August 1949, Kim was whispering in Soviet ears. He and Pak lobbied Ambassador Shtykov, trying to coax first him, then Stalin, into giving the green light. At first, Moscow hesitated. Without a Southern provocation, war was too risky. All Shtykov dared to contemplate was a minor move to seize the Ongjin Peninsula—South Korean territory severed from the mainland by the 38th parallel. Even that was thoroughly vetoed by Stalin. But Kim wouldn't let go.

Then came a turning point. By New Year 1950, Mao had conquered nearly all of China, pushing Chiang Kai-shek to Taiwan. Communism seemed to be sweeping East Asia. On 17 January, a slightly inebriated Kim Il-sung poured his heart out to Soviet officials, declaring that the liberation of the South was a must. This time, the wind was in his favour. Stalin, fresh from talks with the Chinese delegation in Moscow, was more receptive. On 30 January, he cautiously authorised secret preparations. Even Mao wasn't told—yet.

Kim Il-sung, thrilled by the Father of the Nations' blessing, rushed to Moscow in March. For nearly a month, he and his team—among them Pak Hon-yong and Kim's devious secretary Mun Il—hammered out invasion plans with Soviet advisers. In April, Stalin finally let Mao in. Mao pledged support: if the Americans intervened, China would send troops.

By May, the inner circle in Pyongyang was expanding. Kim convened his top brass—Defence Minister Choe Yong-gon, Justice Minister Lee Sung-yop and others—to outline the plan. Only Choe voiced doubts, fearing a US response. But the date was set: Sunday 25 June. Despite Soviet concerns over readiness, Kim insisted on a June launch to beat the summer rains.

On 15 June, the die was cast. North Korean forces moved into position. On 24 June, final orders went out. At dawn the next day, backed by Soviet planners and Chinese guarantees, Kim Il-sung unleashed the war he had begged, bullied and schemed into existence—one that would consume the peninsula and shake global history.

At 4:40 a.m. Seoul time, South Korea was hit with a massive surprise attack. It took the South's army over four hours to even reach the President. According to his secretary, Syngman Rhee was enjoying his usual Sunday fishing session in one of Seoul's palace gardens, blissfully unaware that war had arrived.

That night, Kim summoned his Cabinet and other high-ranking officials for an emergency meeting. Once assembled, he declared that the South had attacked first and that the North was responding with a counteroffensive. The elite, unsurprisingly, backed Kim's claim without question. The lie of Southern aggression has remained North Korea's official narrative ever since.

In those early days, Pyongyang's leadership believed victory would come swiftly. The plan: seize Seoul, spark a mass rebellion, topple Rhee's regime and unify Korea under the DPRK flag. The North had already designated Seoul its capital in the 1948 Constitution. And indeed, with its Soviet-supplied firepower, the North Korean army quickly proved superior. As it approached Seoul, panic spread. Civilians fled; chaos reigned. Seoul fell on 28 June.

Kim Il-sung issued a proclamation to the 'liberated capital of the DPRK', though the regime chose to stay in

Pyongyang. Instead, Kim sent Lee Sung-yop to govern the fallen city. The troops, ordered to rest for three days after taking Seoul, began celebrating rather than pushing forward.

But cracks were appearing. Pyongyang had deluded itself. The South Korean public did not cheer for 'Commander Kim Il-sung'—and the Americans did not abandon the South.

Within days, US planes began bombing the North. The shock of American intervention rattled the Pyongyang elite. By early July, doubts had crept in. Officials began pestering Kim, demanding intervention from China or the USSR. Kim, already on edge, scolded them for fuelling his anxiety.

By mid-August, though, he knew things had gone badly wrong. His secretary told Soviet contacts that he had never seen Kim so shaken. The Southern front refused to collapse, and an American invasion loomed. By late August, Kim privately admitted he wasn't sure North Korea could win. He wanted Chinese help.

Then came the hammer blow.

On 15 September, UN forces led by the United States launched an amphibious landing at Inchon, the port of Seoul. It was a strike of overwhelming power. North Korean defenders were nearly obliterated and, as UN troops surged inland, Kim realised that North Korea, standing alone, was finished. On 21 September, Pyongyang formally requested Chinese support.

MACARTHUR'S TRIUMPH

A week later, on 28 September, Seoul was retaken. The following day, President Rhee triumphantly returned. General MacArthur, commanding the UN forces, declared Seoul South Korean once again. But the war wasn't over. The UN command decided to press on—to bring the battle northward.

By 1 October, as Stalin grimly assessed it: 'The situation of the Korean comrades is getting desperate.'

It was a moment of cold dread. North Korea's fate now rested on a single thread—China. And the only man who could decide to pull on that thread was Mao Zedong.

On 1 October, Stalin, too, formally asked Beijing to intervene. He said that at least five or six divisions—officially branded as 'volunteers'—would be needed to cover the retreating Korean People's Army and give it time to regroup. He expected resistance from Mao and, tellingly, hadn't informed Pyongyang.

Indeed, Mao hesitated. Provoking America directly seemed a dangerous gamble for a country that had just emerged from a devastating civil war. On 2 October, the fateful reply arrived: China would not intervene.

The message was blunt: a few divisions wouldn't turn the tide, declared the Great Helmsman. Marching into Korea risked igniting a world war with the United States. China's fragile recovery would be derailed and, Mao added, the Chinese people wouldn't support such recklessness. His conclusion was chilling: the DPRK would have to endure a 'temporary defeat' and, if needed, resort to guerrilla warfare.

In Moscow, heads were scratched. Just months earlier, Mao had pledged intervention. Now he insisted that the People's Liberation Army was too weak, the risks too high. Soviet Ambassador Nikolai Roschin concluded that Mao had been swayed by the shifting international climate—and by pressure from the West, relayed via Indian intermediaries, urging Beijing to stay out.

North Korea's police chief, Pak Ir-u—a Korean with deep ties to China—travelled to Beijing. He and Mao spoke for ten hours. But Mao was firm. 'I'll help with what I can, but I cannot send the army,' he said. He reasoned that marching into Korea could spark a Third World War. Kim Il-sung, he suggested, should instead retreat to Manchuria and wage a partisan campaign from there.

Truth be told, Mao's logic wasn't easy to dismiss. Launching another brutal war might have been suicidal. His caution seemed prudent—even wise. And without China's backing, North Korea's chances of survival were near zero. History very nearly ended there for the DPRK.

But then, a shift.

Pressure mounted in Beijing—not from Washington, but from Stalin. On 8 October, at six in the morning, a telegram arrived in Pyongyang: China would help. The mood flipped from despair to joy; Kim and Pak Hon-yong celebrated. But the celebration was premature.

In Beijing, the debate was still raging. Vice-Chairman Gao Gang backed intervention. Mao remained sceptical.

Four days later, on 12 October, he told Moscow he had changed his mind again: no troops would be sent.

Stalin's patience snapped. He ordered Kim to prepare for evacuation. But then something changed. Zhou Enlai was in Moscow. When Stalin met him, the Soviet leader was blunt: the USSR supported Chinese intervention—and would assist.

It was the final push. On 13 October, Mao relented, and the wheels were put in motion. North Korea would live another day.

The Chinese army—at enormous cost, and to the deep frustration of its commander, Peng Dehuai, who either knew or suspected who had started the war—recaptured the North. After Stalin's death in 1953, an armistice was signed. The new demarcation line has divided Korea ever since.

For that one week in October, the DPRK's very existence had hung by a thread. It was a coin toss between survival and oblivion. Let's rewind to that razor's-edge week: what if Mao had stuck with his original 'no'?

This alternate history may be one of the most tantalising in this entire book. Unlike many 'what-ifs', this one is grounded in real planning. Back in October 1950, officials on both sides were already bracing for a South Korean victory. We have documents. We know what was set to happen.

On 6 October, as defeat loomed large, Kim Il-sung summoned his trusted secretary Mun Il and laid out a desperate scheme. Mun relayed it to the Soviets, and thus it was recorded for posterity. The plan? Retreat into the mountains, muster a million-strong army—Northerners and Southerners—and launch a counteroffensive after six months or a year to reclaim the nation.

To put it bluntly: fantasy. The proposed force would have dwarfed even the Korean People's Army at its wartime peak—about four times over, in fact. The vision was pure wishful thinking, yet the North Korean Politburo largely approved it. Lee Sung-yop was tapped to lead the southern partisan effort, Pak Ir-u the northern one.

Stalin, however, saw the writing on the wall. He ordered evacuation. Kim Il-sung was to flee, along with every Soviet citizen. A comeback? Maybe—but only if China committed troops, and fully.

Meanwhile, in Pyongyang on 29 October, President Rhee delivered what sounded like a victory speech. The Chinese counteroffensive had yet to be detected, and Rhee was already talking about local elections and a transition to civilian governance in the North. It was bold, but plausible: South Korea had already started forming local administrations in newly captured regions. Historical precedent shows it could have worked—surely, but slowly. After the Korean War, places like Sokcho (seized from the North) were initially run by the US Army and only fully integrated into the Republic of Korea sixteen months later.

Rhee's vision was inclusive: no discrimination against those who lived under the Communists. 'If anyone now tries to divide us into "Southerners" or "Northerners", mark them as enemies of the future of the Republic of Korea and condemn them,' he declared. He promised rice, fabric and shelter. 'Never again will any country divide us!' Rhee thundered.

So—what if it had ended there? If you're looking for a haunting glimpse into what might have become of Kim Il-sung and his inner circle without China's intervention, look no further than a man from a very different corner of the world: Nikos Zachariadis, the fiery General Secretary of the Greek Communist Party.

Like Kim, Zachariadis was no mere ideologue—he was a man of action, launching the Greek Civil War in the late 1940s with dreams of turning Greece red. Dreams can die hard: when his Democratic Army was crushed by Western-backed government forces, the revolutionary fled to the Soviet Union, clinging to the hope of one day returning to create a guerrilla underground inside Greece. But hope is not enough. Zachariadis' plans for a partisan revival were quietly strangled by the efficiency of Greece's Central Intelligence Service, which proved adept at mopping up what was left of the Communist underground.

The final blow came not from Athens, but from Moscow. When Khrushchev denounced Stalin in 1956, the exiled Greek Communist Party smelled blood. They gathered in plenum and expelled their former leader, declaring him an enemy of the cause. The Soviets were only too pleased to help. Zachariadis was exiled from Moscow and eventually sent off to a remote corner of West Siberia, effectively abandoned both by the movement he had once led and the country that had become his shelter.

There in Siberia, far from the battlefields of his youth and the politics of his homeland, Zachariadis faded into obscurity. He petitioned, pleaded, tried for years to reclaim his name—to no avail. In 1973, forgotten and broken, he hanged himself. The cruel twist? Just a year later, democratic reforms in Greece allowed Communists to return home and take part in political life. They entered Parliament, yes—but they never managed to win even 10 per cent of the seats.

Perhaps, in another world, this was the sort of fate that could have befallen Kim Il-sung: exile in the Soviet Union or, more likely, in familiar Northeast China; desperate attempts to organise an underground struggle against a victorious Seoul—echoing Kim's 1930s guerrilla days in colonial Korea. Inevitably, his underground would be crushed, leaving him to drift in the shadows. Beyond that, the picture blurs: would Kim have suffered a Siberian exile like Zachariadis? Or become a victim of China's Cultural Revolution purges in the 1960s and '70s? Depression, betrayal, anonymity—history's darker shadows close in.

And what of his fellow Communists? Should a reunited Korea have veered toward the democratic model of the South which we know today, might the Communists, like their Greek comrades, have returned decades later to a political arena where they'd once failed to hold on to power?

History is full of such ghost roads—futures that never came to pass. But in October 1950, for a fleeting moment, the fall of Kim Il-sung wasn't just a fantasy. It was nearly fact.

The shockwaves of such a defeat would have echoed far beyond Korea's jagged hills—rippling all the way back to the heart of American power. Picture General Douglas MacArthur, already lionised for his bold defence of South Korea's southern tip, soaring into near-mythic stature. His public approval would have soared as triumphant images of his troops flooded newspapers and newsreels.

MacArthur's already gilded reputation would have demanded the highest military honour: the elusive sixth star, elevating him to General of the Armies—a rank no living American held, placing him above every uniformed figure in the nation. For context, the Greek General Alexandros Papagos, who secured victory in Greece's Civil War, was awarded the exceptional rank of Field Marshal.

In reality, MacArthur was already a contender for the 1952 Republican Presidential nomination. After triumphing in Korea, his chances would have surged, perhaps even eclipsing Dwight D. Eisenhower. Given the GOP's dominance at the time, a MacArthur presidency would then have seemed almost certain.

The political reverberations? Monumental. The Civil Rights Movement, the course of American society—all could have been reshaped. Consider Richard Nixon's rise, fuelled by his role as Eisenhower's running mate and later architect of the Southern Strategy. A victorious MacArthur might have rerouted this political path in ways impossible to predict.

To say that the Korean War's outcome could have transformed not only Korea but also the United States—and, by extension, the entire world—is no exaggeration. The ripples from that one moment would have echoed through history, altering the political and social fabric of the twentieth century forever.

6

The Opposition Wins
In 1956, Kim Il-sung could have been voted out of office

Long before the guns fell silent in the Korean War, Kim Il-sung was already eyeing his real battlefield: the corridors of power. He was playing a long game, one measured not in days but in decades, and carefully stacking North Korea's top institutions with handpicked loyalists. It was a calculated move to eliminate any chance that the elite might one day rise against him.

After all, Kim himself had been installed by the Soviets, and the first North Korean leadership had been assembled on Moscow's terms. Four distinct groups made up this initial ruling class. First, the local revolutionaries—underground activists who had resisted Japanese colonial rule from within Korea, most of them hailing from Seoul, and now irrevocably severed from the South by the demarcation line. Then came the Soviet Koreans—ethnic Koreans deported en masse from the Soviet Far East to Central Asia in 1937, suspected by Stalin of harbouring loyalties to Tokyo. Yet, by 1945, these same people were being called back to serve the newborn North Korean state, often in startlingly high positions. Nam Il, once a minor education official, became Chief of Staff—a meteoric rise by any measure.

Among the Soviet Koreans were former Comintern agents, some of whom had been freed from Japanese prisons by the Red Army and swiftly absorbed into Pyongyang's apparatus. Then there were the Chinese Koreans, closely tied to the Chinese Communist Party. Lastly—and most trusted of all—came Kim's own comrades, men who had served alongside him in the Manchurian guerrilla struggle and later in the Soviet 88th Brigade.

By default, Kim placed his faith only in the last group. Others could earn his trust, but only through unwavering loyalty. One notable example was Pang Hak-se, a Soviet Korean who rose to command the feared state security apparatus—a rare outsider admitted into the inner sanctum.

The rule was simple, brutal, and absolute: if you weren't one of Kim's own, you were out. The first man to detect this shift was his own secretary, Mun Il. A Soviet Korean, Mun was a spectral figure in North Korea's early years. His fingerprints are all over the founding moments of the regime: he recommended Kim Il-sung to the Soviets, introduced him to Soviet generals in Pyongyang back in '45, and was among the first to whisper in '49 that perhaps, just perhaps, invading the South wasn't such a mad idea after all.

THE OPPOSITION WINS

But Mun was also the first to flee—sensing, with eerie foresight, that remaining close to Kim could be fatal.

The purges came swiftly. First to fall were the so-called 'domestic' revolutionaries—those without a foreign Communist patron to protect them. Justice Minister Lee Sung-yop, once appointed by Kim himself to govern Seoul, was suddenly branded a traitor and executed. Next was Pak Hon-yong, Kim's former deputy and a key architect of the Korean War. Accused of being an American spy, he rotted in prison before facing the firing squad.

Aleksei Hegay, perhaps the most powerful Soviet Korean in the country, was publicly shamed, stripped of his position as Party Vice-Chairman, demoted to Vice-Premier, and then—after yet another round of harsh criticism—found dead in his home. Officially, it was suicide. Perhaps it truly was—Hegay's father had taken his own life, and Aleksei's final visit to the Soviet embassy showed him visibly despondent. But his family never believed it, convinced that Kim Il-sung had had him killed.

Then came Pak Ir-u, the Chinese-aligned Minister of Internal Affairs. His ties to Beijing had grown stronger during the war. He too was arrested. The purge list lengthened by the day.

The only serious challenge to Kim Il-sung's tightening grip came from Vice-Premier Pak Chang-ok—a Soviet Korean, bold, cunning and, in many ways, a mirror of Kim himself. At the time, Kim occupied two thrones: Chairman of the Central Committee and Premier. In 1955, Pak dared to propose that no single man should wield both. It was a perfectly sound suggestion—power-sharing had become gospel in Moscow after Stalin's death. Across Eastern Europe, strongmen were being humbled: Bulgaria's Chervenkov, Hungary's Rákosi, even Albania's iron-fisted Hoxha had been forced to surrender one of their crowns.

But Kim Il-sung played by different rules. He stalled, manoeuvred and, with impeccable tactical flair, nominated the wildly unpopular Defence Minister Choe Yong-gon as his own replacement. Faced with a choice, the elite blinked—and opted for the devil they knew.

It seemed that Kim Il-sung had outmanoeuvred them all. But just as the dust began to settle, a political earthquake struck—a 10 on the Richter scale.

On 25 February 1956, Nikita Khrushchev stood before the Soviet Congress and denounced Stalin. The man the entire Communist world had worshipped as a god was now branded a cruel and petty tyrant; his cult declared a stain on the cause. The message was clear: Stalin's heirs across the Eastern Bloc—those who ruled in his image—were suddenly vulnerable. Including Kim Il-sung.

By the spring of 1956, discontent simmered in the backrooms of Pyongyang. A plot was forming, one that— had it succeeded—might have rewritten Korean history. Its unlikely spearhead was Choe Chang-ik, a grizzled Communist with one decade of revolutionary grit earned in

THE OPPOSITION WINS

Mao's Chinese underground and another in Pyongyang's cabinets. Alongside him stood an uneasy alliance of disgruntled officials, would-be reformers, schemers, and bitter men with long memories. Their aim was audacious: topple Kim Il-sung.

What united them? Ambition, ideology, frustration—and, perhaps, pride. Ironically, some had once helped Kim eliminate his rivals. Now, they struck a temporary alliance, hoping to do the same to him. But dreams require discipline, and this cabal had none.

Timing was everything. With Stalin's ghost on trial and found guilty, Kim knew the tide might turn against him. But he kept his cool. As he remarked during a visit to Mongolia that year, 'I used to be quite hasty and brisk in my youth, but with age, that is no longer the case.' Instead of defending himself, he deflected. Yes, there had been a cult—but the culprit, he claimed, was Pak Hon-yong, long since purged. Problem solved.

The opposition didn't buy it. But they weren't ready. North Korea was about to hold a Party Congress in April—an event where the Central Committee would be elected, the body with the power to remove the Chairman.

Kim Il-sung came prepared. His loyalists secured key positions; dissident voices were censored. One bold outlier—Lee Sang-jo, North Korea's ambassador to Moscow—submitted a note demanding a formal debate on the leadership cult. He was never allowed to speak.

As the Third Congress ended, it was obvious who had won. No critical speeches were permitted. Kim was re-elected Chairman without a hitch. In quiet conversations, some still called him 'Master', echoing Stalin's old nickname.

The plotters weren't finished. They planned to challenge Kim at a new Central Committee plenum. But they had far too few votes—thirty-six were needed, and they came up short. Worse, after the Congress, half of the Committee were new faces—spineless, loyal to Kim, or simply bought. Even inside the opposition's own camp, courage was thin. Some hoped that mild criticism might be enough to make Kim change course.

In truth, their only hope lay in the Soviet Union. But, instead of quietly courting Moscow, they blundered. They grumbled in public and confronted Kim openly. They shouted when they should have whispered. Kim, a master manipulator, watched and listened. And planned.

After the Congress, he wasn't sure when the next blow would come. But, while visiting the Soviet Union, he was scolded by the Kremlin. The threat was real. He returned home promising reforms, while quietly readying his defences. The police were mobilised. Allies were briefed. Enemies were watched, pressured, or both.

Eventually, the plotters did what they should have done earlier: they talked to the Soviets. On 8 June, Choe Chang-ik aired his grievances to Ambassador Ivanov, though he stopped short of calling for Kim's removal. Others were

THE OPPOSITION WINS

bolder—Lee Sang-jo reported the full plot to Moscow by early August, including a plan to appoint Choe Chang-ik as Party Chairman and Defence Minister Choe Yong-gon as Supreme Commander. They hoped the latter, Kim's old comrade, would switch sides.

He didn't.

Now came the final act. It was a Thursday. On 30 August, the Central Committee Hall in Pyongyang crackled with tension. The knives were out, the Leader ready, history watching.

Kim opened with a breezy travelogue from his Soviet tour, brushing aside the 'cult of personality' as a solved issue. Then Trade Minister Yun Kong-hum rose and launched a bold attack—accusing Kim of hypocrisy, vanity and silencing a nation in favour of one man's ideas.

He was swiftly drowned out as Kim's loyalists erupted. The room became a battleground of slurs and shouting. Defence Minister Choe led the charge. Kim called a vote: should Yun be allowed to finish? Only seven dared say yes.

Yun fled the hall. Kim proposed his expulsion from the Committee for being absent. Only So Hwi, the union boss, voted no. He would be remembered as the last liberal voice in North Korea.

By dawn, Yun, So and two others had fled—racing towards the Chinese border in a borrowed car. Mao took them in; they survived. The rest remained behind, trapped beneath the shadow of the man they had dared to confront.

Those who failed to escape were either shot or died in prison camps, leaving Kim Il-sung the unchallenged ruler.

The question now arises—what if the opposition had been smarter? Suppose they had approached Ivanov much earlier and persuaded the Ambassador to send a report to Khrushchev, urging Kim Il-sung's dismissal? *Chairman Kim, at heart, remains a Stalinist and will never embrace the new line on his own.* Imagine they had kept the conspiracy secret, smiling at Kim Il-sung in every meeting, nodding enthusiastically at his proposals, while quietly assuring the doubters that Moscow was on their side. What might have happened if, as Yun Kong-hum intended, the Central Committee had condemned Kim Il-sung's cult, then moved to dismiss him, installing Comrade Choe Chang-ik as his successor?

The rise of Choe would almost certainly have set North Korea on the path to becoming a full-blown Maoist state. In 1956, Chinese troops remained stationed on Korean soil, and with a pro-Chinese leader at the helm, that 'temporary' arrangement could easily have become permanent. The Americans had entrenched themselves in the South with the 1954 mutual defence treaty. Why shouldn't Pyongyang argue that Chinese forces were needed to counterbalance US imperialism?

But, soon enough, the Communist world would be rocked by the Sino-Soviet split—and had the Chinese-aligned faction seized control in Pyongyang, Soviet

THE OPPOSITION WINS

Koreans would have been living on borrowed time. Even if the fragile coalition that carried Choe Chang-ik to power had somehow held together after Kim's removal, the schism between the two Communist titans would have spelled its inevitable doom. The actual mass exodus of Soviet Koreans that began in the late 1950s could only have been postponed by a few years. Heavyweights of Soviet origin, such as Pak Chang-ok and Pak Ui-wan, would likely still have faced the purge, having failed to flee while the exits were still open.

A Maoist North Korea would have meant plunging headfirst into the nightmare that Mao had already prepared for China: the Great Leap Forward, followed by the Cultural Revolution. That would have entailed the continuation—and even intensification—of Kim Il-sung's brutal policies of forced collectivisation and reckless industrialisation. The already precarious agricultural sector would have been battered further, possibly tipping the nation into widespread famine. The horrors of China's mass starvation might have played out again, this time on Korean soil.

Then would come the purges. The chaos of the Cultural Revolution—with its public humiliations and beatings—would likely have been mirrored in Pyongyang. Anyone accused of insufficient loyalty to the Leader might have found themselves denounced by neighbours, dragged through the streets, or torn apart by mobs of Chairman Choe's loyalist zealots.

Even language might not have escaped untouched. During this era, Mao famously simplified Chinese characters—and one can readily imagine a Maoist North Korea embarking on its own linguistic revolution. Perhaps the mixed Korean script would have been revived: grammar and native terms written in the Korean alphabet, with the Chinese-derived words (an estimated 70 per cent of Korean vocabulary) written in simplified Chinese characters. A bold symbol of a 'new era'. The Korean language, already rich with Sino-linguistic influence, might have grown even more Sinified, with the Pyongyang dialect awash in Chinese vocabulary. Scholars in both countries could have marvelled that Mao's 'Red Guards' and Choe's equivalent were written with the same characters: Hongweibing in China, Hongwibyong in Korea.

And what of Kim Il-sung in this alternate world? His fate would have been grim indeed. Even if Choe had chosen to spare his life—an unlikely mercy—Kim would have made an irresistible target for the Hongwibyong. One can imagine the spectacle: the once-mighty Marshal dragged from his home, a yoke hung round his neck inscribed with a slogan in mixed script, forced to kneel in the dust and beg for forgiveness. This was the Red Guards' ritual humiliation of enemies of the Great Helmsman in China—and North Korea's own fanatics would have taken no less glee in meting it out. Kim Il-sung might have been branded a 'pro-Soviet element' and a 'capitalist roader'—the standard Maoist insults for revisionists, thrown at a man who, in reality, loathed Khrushchev and his reforms. The former Premier would almost certainly have suffered unpleasant flashbacks to the 1930s, when partisan comrades had falsely accused him of joining a pro-Japanese organisation, and he had been forced to plead guilty in order to save his life.

As for the distant future? It's tempting to imagine Choe's North Korea eventually following its Chinese patron down the path of reform and openness. After all, Choe was only three years Mao's junior and might well have died around the same time. But that future lies deep in the mist of speculation. What is clearer is this: the Kim–Choe showdown of August 1956—so often misread as a clash between a hardliner and a moderate—was anything but that. Had Choe Chang-ik triumphed, North Korea's suffering would not have eased. It would simply have changed its flavour. The masses would still have faced tyranny and terror—just in a different shade, with any hope for improvement possibly emerging only decades later, most likely once the leader of the coup himself had gone to his grave.

7

Red Giants Crush a Small Sun
Sino-Soviet political intervention could have removed Kim Il-sung from power in 1956

In 1956, Kim Il-sung endured two political crises mere weeks apart—so tightly packed that one might be forgiven for lumping them together. Yet each carried wholly different stakes for the future of North Korea.

The first was the August plenum, covered in the previous chapter. The second arrived almost immediately thereafter: a joint Sino-Soviet intervention in its wake. In September 1956, Pyongyang found itself hosting Soviet Deputy Premier Anastas Mikoyan and Chinese Marshal Peng Dehuai—once commander of Chinese forces in Korea.

A surprisingly unlikely figure set this intervention in motion: Lee Sang-jo, North Korea's ambassador to the USSR. Born in colonial Korea in 1916, Lee, too, had joined the anti-Japanese movement in Manchuria, but was never a partisan like Kim Il-sung. Later he became one of the earliest members of the Workers' Party and climbed to top positions in both Party and military during the Korean War. Although lacking battlefield experience, he had served as Deputy Chief of Staff and played a pivotal role in armistice negotiations. In 1955, he was posted to Moscow, where he embraced Soviet life and grew increasingly disillusioned with Kim Il-sung's escalating cult.

Inspired by Khrushchev's 'Secret Speech' denouncing Stalin in February 1956, Lee attempted to criticise Kim at the Party Congress in April—only to be sidelined. Kim could have had him arrested, but feared that jailing his own ambassador to Moscow would draw unwelcome scrutiny from the Kremlin. Instead, Lee Sang-jo was allowed to return to the USSR, which stranded him in Moscow during Pyongyang's August plenum.

When news reached Lee that his comrades had failed to curb Kim Il-sung's power, he refused to accept defeat. Instead, he penned a boldly conceived—though cautiously worded—letter to Khrushchev himself: a plea for justice, a protest against comrades expelled merely for speaking their minds, and a hint that affairs in North Korea were careering out of control. Lee floated several remedies, the most audacious being a request for a Soviet emissary to fly to Pyongyang, reassess the plenum's decisions and 'correct' its mistakes.

Even so, Lee hesitated to call outright for Kim's removal. Torn between ideological loyalty and grim political reality, he still clung to the hope that this was all a misunderstanding among comrades. Perhaps fraternal criticism would guide Kim back to the straight and narrow.

Khrushchev listened. He swiftly conferred with Mao Zedong—who was also infuriated by recent purges of Chinese Koreans in Pyongyang—and agreed to co-ordinate an intervention. Initially, they considered summoning Kim to Beijing for talks, but Kim demurred, claiming ill health. Instead, a high-profile delegation was assembled: Mikoyan, Khrushchev's wily deputy, and the formidable Marshal Peng Dehuai, still nursing old grudges against Kim for having ignited the Korean War.

However, this joint Sino-Soviet team arrived in Pyongyang without a detailed script. It appears that Khrushchev had echoed Lee's broad suggestion, charging Mikoyan and Peng only with discovering what was happening in Pyongyang and ensuring that the August Plenum's 'mistakes' were rectified. Mao, too, balked at backing an outright removal of Kim—fearing it might unleash a power struggle within the North Korean elite. Nevertheless, they departed to Pyongyang with a clear message: Kim had overreached.

Tension crackled in the air as the two emissaries met the North Korean Chairman face to face. The outcome was a partial backtrack: under the watchful gaze of Moscow and Beijing, a new Party Plenum convened in September 1956. A handful of comrades were rehabilitated—but only to a point. Choe Chang-ik, the most dangerous of the dissenters, was readmitted to the Central Committee but remained barred from its Presidium, where true power laid. Mikoyan likely toyed with calling for Kim's removal altogether, only to be deterred upon surveying the newly stacked Central Committee: 'It may cause a split, for everyone was "in support". Someday, but not now,' reads a line in Mikoyan's hurried, handwritten notes.

Kim, ever the strategist, grasped the game. Faced with overwhelming pressure, he conceded—just enough to survive. Then, as his adversaries' eyes turned elsewhere, he struck back. This ploy was nothing new; he had refined it in Manchuria, where feigned submission to Party authority had often saved him from purges. The ruse worked once more: the storm subsided, and the very men who'd tried to muzzle him instead unwittingly cemented his claim to power. In stark irony, the twin crises of 1956—born of daring conspiracies and frantic diplomacy—concluded not with Kim's downfall, but his coronation.

A few months later, Kim resumed purging the opposition. The new Soviet ambassador, the inept bureaucrat Aleksandr Puzanov—exiled to Pyongyang by Khrushchev—offered no protest, no initiative. Still, Moscow tried to press Kim: he must restore collective leadership, relinquish either the Party Chairmanship or the Premiership. Kim stalled, unfazed. As Khrushchev moved to centralise power in mid-1957, collective leadership fell from favour. Sensing the shift, Kim consolidated his grip: the new cabinet placed him firmly at its head.

That gamble paid off handsomely—retribution never came. Once Kim realised he could simply ignore Moscow, the Kremlin's sway over North Korea crumbled. By the early 1960s, Kim Il-sung reigned supreme, unchallenged and unbowed.

Perhaps the most fascinating—if heart-breaking—aspect of the 1956 crisis is just how narrowly North Korea missed its one real chance for change. Had Lee Sang-jo been a little less idealistic, had he dared to write plainly to Moscow that the only viable solution was Kim Il-sung's removal, history might have turned on its heel. Khrushchev, already leaning in that direction, would almost certainly have backed such a course. Mao would likely have gone along, harbouring as he did his own deep grievances—Kim had, after all, dragged China into war in 1950, then purged the very pro-Chinese officials who had stood by him.

With the combined will of Moscow and Beijing behind them, Mikoyan and Peng would not have needed tanks or bayonets. A proclamation may have sufficed, along the lines of 'the joint opinion of the CPSU and the CCP is that Comrade Kim Il-sung should step down', paired with a carefully sharpened hint about what disobedience might provoke—especially with Chinese troops still stationed in the North. Faced with that kind of pressure, North Korea's elite, already shaken by the delegation's arrival, could have crumbled. One formal vote, and Chairman Kim might have been history.

Had Kim Il-sung been forced to resign, as some once dared to hope, the fate of North Korea would have fallen into the hands of two outsiders: Anastas Mikoyan and Peng Dehuai. But let's not pretend the choice would have been equal. In 1956, the Soviet Union still held the reins of influence, and Mikoyan would almost certainly have rung up Khrushchev for marching orders.

And so, our road not taken splits at its very beginning. For in Moscow's pocket there were two contenders for the throne: Vice-Premiers Pak Chang-ok and Pak Ui-wan. They shared a surname, pre-confrontation membership of the Central Committee's Presidium, and a Soviet background—but little else. In fact, they represented two utterly opposed visions for North Korea's future.

If there was a man in Pyongyang's elite who mirrored Kim Il-sung in temperament and ambition, it was surely Pak Chang-ok. A former military intelligence operative, Pak had weathered danger and hardship like Kim—and emerged just as hungry for power. It was Pak, after all, who had dared suggest Kim's removal in 1955. No one else had ever so directly challenged the Supreme Leader.

So, what might a Korea ruled by Pak Chang-ok have looked like? One suspects he'd have wasted no time purging rivals—Kim Il-sung among them—along with any former allies who'd outlived their usefulness. Initially, he'd have followed Moscow's reformist line, at least outwardly. But, as Kim did in reality, Pak might well have shrugged off Soviet oversight the moment it suited him. He had the cunning. He had the nerve.

And what a chilling prospect that is. Imagine a Pak-led Korea playing Moscow off against Beijing during the Sino-Soviet split, just as Kim would. Imagine another decades-long dictatorship, built on propaganda, repression and fear. Pak had already proven his flair for falsehoods—he was instrumental in concocting the claim that the United States used bioweapons during the Korean War. Power-hungry, manipulative and deeply paranoid, but with a soft spot for his son Pak Il-san—an eerie parallel to Kim's grooming of Kim Jong-il—Pak might have driven Korea down a very familiar, very grim path.

Now consider his opposite: Pak Ui-wan. While his rival schemed and climbed, this Pak managed railways and factories, preaching frugality and decency in a political culture that rewarded neither. He once scolded a factory director for gifting his family a set of furniture. When his wife protested—it was hardly a luxury—he pointed out of the window toward a city of dugouts and told her, with tears in his eyes, to compare.

Idealistic and incorruptible, Pak Ui-wan was ill-suited to a system built on intrigue. And yet, had Mikoyan installed him, we might have glimpsed a radically different North Korea. True, he would have ruled by Soviet fiat, and the precedent of Kim's removal would have hung over him like a sword. One misstep into liberalism and he might have shared the fate of Imre Nagy or Alexander Dubček.

But imagine if he'd pulled it off. With his concern for the poor and his background in economic management, Pak might have shifted the regime's focus from guns to grain, from hollow slogans to functioning railroads. North Korea under his watch could have moved toward economic rationality, investing in food, medicine and infrastructure instead of endless military development. Perhaps even political reforms would have followed—multi-candidate local elections, a softer surveillance state.

During China's Great Leap Forward and Cultural Revolution, a humane North Korea under Pak Ui-wan might have opened its doors to Chinese refugees, expanding the diaspora and planting seeds of cross-border empathy rarely seen in that part of the world.

And what of the country's name? The mouthful 'Democratic People's Republic of Korea' might not have survived. Between 1960 and 1976, many Communist states swapped their 'people's' and 'democratic' labels for 'socialist', signalling progress beyond the transitional phase. Kim, never one for ideological niceties, left the name alone. But under a Soviet ally like Pak Ui-wan or even Pak Chang-ok, the country could have been renamed to 'Korean Socialist Republic'.

So here we stand, looking at a historical crossroads. One path leads to a grim mirror of what truly came to pass. The other, to a fragile hope—a North Korea that might have chosen bread over bombs, and decency over fear.

8

Pyongyang's Gamble, Seoul's Victory?
Kim Il-sung could have killed President Park Chung-hee and launched the Second Korean War

The concept of a 'second Korean War' isn't confined to the realms of old war plans or alternate-history fiction. In fact, it was a term coined to describe a turbulent period in the late 1960s, when tensions on the Korean Peninsula reached extraordinary heights. Inspired by North Vietnam's success in its struggle against the US, Kim Il-sung sought to destabilise the South by any means necessary.

His tactics were relentless and diverse. Special commando teams infiltrated South Korea in a series of attempts (always unsuccessful) to create 'liberated zones' on the southern side of the border. But the provocations didn't stop there. In 1968, the USS *Pueblo*, an American spy ship, was captured by North Korean forces. The following year, in 1969, an EC-121 reconnaissance plane was shot down, killing all thirty-one American crew members aboard. That same year, a South Korean civilian airliner was hijacked by North Korean agents.

The drama continued to unfold, but it wasn't until 2010 that the true extent of Kim Il-sung's ambitions came to light. In that year, Chinese scholar Cheng Xiaohe unveiled a startling document that had remained hidden for decades. The document revealed that, in 1965, Kim had confided in the Chinese ambassador, Hao Deqing. Kim declared that a South Korean uprising was imminent and, as he put it, 'We ask your army to participate in the future conflict!' This revelation, a kind of smoking gun, confirms what historians had long suspected: after the armistice of 1953, Kim wanted a rematch, and was planning a second invasion of the South.

Kim's fixation on heavy industry, on rapid development of paramilitaries, the expanded length of national service—it all made sense if one knew the Premier was thinking about an aggressive war. Even after failing to secure China's support, Kim Il-sung never abandoned his dream, planning for more operations, hoping that perhaps Seoul would start to crumble.

There was a single time when one of his plans came so close to success that it is very tempting to consider how the events would have unfurled thereafter. It happened in January 1968, when Kim Il-sung ordered the dispatch of an elite commando team with an order to kill the President of South Korea, Park Chung-hee.

The task—as Kim Il-sung put it in his official order, to 'bring here the head of the seditious puppet'—fell upon a group that, in typical North Korean fashion, was given only a number: Unit 124. On 16 January 1968, the unit departed in six vehicles, heading toward the Demilitarised Zone. By the 18th, they had reached the Military Demarcation Line separating the two Koreas; the following day saw them crossing the Imjin River under cover. While deep behind enemy lines, they encountered four brothers chopping wood. In a fatal display of overconfidence, they revealed their identity as members of the Korean People's Army.

One of the woodcutters quickly feigned loyalty, presenting himself and his brothers as poor labourers yearning for unification under the banner of the DPRK. The ruse worked, and a vote among the infiltrators spared the brothers—the effort of hiding the bodies in this mountainous terrain was deemed too great. Before letting them go, the operatives issued a chilling ultimatum: 'If you report this, your entire family will be slaughtered.'

Back home, the brothers made up an excuse about chasing a raccoon. But over dinner, the tension became too much. Trembling, they eventually confessed. Alarmed, the family rushed to a nearby police outpost and raised the alarm. Authorities wasted no time—both South Korean and American forces were alerted, and a high state of readiness was declared.

Yet the true aim of the incursion—the assassination of President Park—had not yet been uncovered. Security around the Blue House remained dangerously lax.

On the night of 21 January, Unit 124 donned civilian attire and concealed their arms beneath long overcoats. By 7 p.m., they had reached the heart of Seoul. Had they been stopped, they might have passed as members of South Korea's own counterintelligence. It was only due to the sharp eyes of local police that the plot began to unravel.

At around 9:55 p.m., a station chief noticed a group of men moving in a loosely organised manner. He hurried to a nearby substation and sent a city-wide alert.

The unit's first checkpoint encounter was with two detectives. At 10:05 p.m., the infiltrators claimed to be military agents returning from an exercise and insisted on passage. The detectives hesitated and called for backup, which arrived shortly thereafter. Just then, two city buses began ascending the road. The North Koreans mistook them for army transports, and panic overtook the group—they believed the buses were full of troops. They launched grenades and opened fire, throwing the scene into chaos.

Most members of the unit were killed in the aftermath. One man—Kim Shin-jo—evaded the cordon and hid in a secluded home. He buried his weapons and kept one grenade—reserved for suicide.

In the early hours of 22 January, at 2:25 a.m., a South Korean unit surrounded the house. After a brief firefight, they tried to negotiate: 'Come out and we'll spare your life.' Kim emerged, grenade in hand. He might have pulled the pin. Instead, he let it fall and gave himself up. Later, he would explain his choice in the plainest words: 'I am a human being, and I wanted to live.'

One can see clearly how close the team came to success. What would have happened if, say, the woodcutter brothers had decided to work somewhere else on that fateful day? What if the team had managed to storm the Blue House and to 'slice Park Chung-hee's throat', as Kim Shin-jo blurted during a press conference, shocking the South Korean public?

For Kim Il-sung, this could easily have signified the 'now or never' moment. With South Korea beheaded, he could have launched his campaign, hoping that China or the Soviet Union—or, better, both—would help him when faced with a fait accompli. In fact, documents and testimonies from the time reveal that this was one of the greatest fears for the Communist Bloc. They were aware of the preparations, and understood that a second North Korean invasion of the South was a very real possibility. Seoul's intelligence estimates and the testimonies of people who had escaped the North show a similar picture. Kim Il-sung himself, in a classified 1969 speech later brought to South Korea by an escaped KPA officer, warned that a 'coup' in Seoul could be the spark that would ignite war.

And what about South Korea? With President Park dead, the next in line would have been Prime Minister Chung Il-kwon. Under the Constitution, he was to assume the role of Acting President and call a new election. The document contained a curious clause: if the Presidency became vacant with less than two years left in the term, the National Assembly would choose a successor. But that provision wouldn't come into effect until May 1969—over a year after the attempted assassination. Park's replacement, then, would have to be chosen by direct vote.

That reality would have stirred hope among the democratic opposition, which had performed strongly in the 1967 election—Yun Po-son, their candidate, won over 40 per cent of the vote. According to the Constitution, the election was to be held 'immediately', with no exceptions made for a state of emergency—even one which Chung would almost certainly have declared upon assuming office.

Here our alternate history immediately enters uncharted territory—there are too many variables to consider. How would Chung Il-kwon proceed? This man was never a person with a particular lust for power, faithfully serving Park and then fawning over Park's authoritarian successor, Chun Doo-hwan. Would he have allowed an election? Would he have run? Would the opposition have stood a chance? Would the new government have been stable—or would it have suffered another coup? And how would a possible North Korean invasion—perhaps a month or two after the assassination—have factored into all of this?

Very soon, the situation would have become even more unpredictable. Just two days after North Korean commandos stormed Seoul in an attempt to reach the Blue House, another crisis erupted: the capture of the American spy ship USS *Pueblo* by the North Korean Navy. Its crew was held for eleven months, sparking fury in Washington. But what if Park had already been dead by the time the ship was taken? What if Kim Il-sung, emboldened by that power vacuum in the South, had been preparing to invade?

From what we know now, the decision to seize the *Pueblo* was taken locally, with Kim informed only after the fact. Yet, in the context of an imminent conflict, releasing the ship and its crew could have been a clever ploy—an illusion of goodwill from a peace-loving Pyongyang. After all, that had been the game in 1950. Pyongyang preached peace, all the while preparing for war.

Had Park been assassinated, South Korea would have plunged into sudden turmoil. The spectre of war would have loomed large over the peninsula. Washington, staring into the abyss, would have had to act fast. Reinforcements would have poured into Korea, likely pulled from Japan and—more dangerously—from South Vietnam.

Just nine days after the attempt on Park's life, North Vietnam unleashed the Tet Offensive—the third major event of that fateful fortnight early in 1968. It was not a single blow, but a storm—co-ordinated attacks on dozens of South Vietnamese cities, including Saigon itself. The Viet Cong were beaten back and bloodied, but that wasn't the true battleground. The real defeat happened in American living rooms.

The offensive shattered the illusion of progress. The war, far from being won, looked endless. The enemy, far from collapsing, seemed relentless. The psychological toll was devastating. And one of its casualties wasn't a soldier—it was the career of the President of the United States.

Lyndon B. Johnson's time in the White House since 1963 had been nothing short of revolutionary. He tore down segregation with the Civil Rights Act and built a new social safety net with Medicare and Medicaid. But Vietnam was the stain no domestic victory could scrub clean. Disillusioned liberals—once his allies—turned away. By March 1968, bruised and politically exhausted, Johnson stunned the nation: he would not seek re-election.

But what if Park had died right before the Tet Offensive was launched? Two Communist assaults in Asia, within days of each other, would have looked more than coincidence, even if, in hindsight, they probably actually were. Would the American public have believed in a wider conspiracy? Would fingers have pointed at Brezhnev or Mao? Would Johnson, instead of stepping down, have been seen as a wartime leader under siege?

That's the trouble with history—it hinges on such delicate threads.

As for the war that might have followed in Korea, it's a puzzle full of unknowns. If Kim Il-sung had moved quickly, he could have struck during South Korea's snap election, seizing the chaos to frame the invasion as a counterattack.

PYONGYANG'S GAMBLE, SEOUL'S VICTORY?

In 1950, Pyongyang had claimed to be the victim. In 1968, this narrative could have returned: 'We were attacked by traitors and launched an immediate counteroffensive.'

If Prime Minister and Acting President Chung Il-kwon had remained in power, North Korean propaganda would have had a field day. Chung wasn't just a South Korean statesman. He was once called Nakajima Ikken—a loyal subject of the Japanese Emperor, an officer in the Imperial Manchurian Army that clashed with Communist partisans like Kim Il-sung. The two never met or interacted, but the contrast would have been striking: 'Comrades! Will you follow Marshal Kim Il-sung, the sun of our liberation, or Chung Il-kwon, the man who sold his countrymen first to Japan, then to the Yankees?'

But would such a war even happen? Would Beijing and Moscow have backed Kim after Park's assassination? From today's declassified materials, it seems they were not prepared to do so. An aggressive war against the South was the worst-case scenario; if it happened, Kim was quite possibly to be left on his own. Yet plans and reality often differ, and no one can know what Brezhnev and Mao would have done if faced with an actual war.

What we do know is this: the attempted assassination of Park Chung-hee had the potential to derail not just Korean history, but the trajectory of the entire world. Had events spiralled differently, by the end of 1968, Earth could have been a very different place indeed.

PART III

DEATH, COUP OR WAR

1990s

9

Shooting the Sun
Kim Il-sung and Kim Jong-il could have been killed in a 1992 coup

Kim Il-sung's grip on North Korea crystallised in the aftermath of the August Plenum and the botched Sino-Soviet attempt to intervene. From that moment, for more than thirty years, the only force that could have undone the Great Leader's reign was his own hubris. Only in the late 1960s, when he flirted with the catastrophic idea of launching a second invasion of South Korea, had he come dangerously close to self-destruction.

Beyond that brief, feverish chapter, the decades that followed were a nightmare wrapped in ritual—what one might call blissful horror. In 1967, Kim declared the Singular Thought System, a doctrine that elevated him from man to demigod. It wasn't enough for North Koreans to simply live in silence. From now on, daily life was to be infused with ritual worship. Every published text had to open with a quote from the Great Leader. Every home was to hang his portrait. Every person had to wear a badge with his likeness. His biography, sliced into the sacred phases of 'Childhood' and 'Revolutionary History', became required reading in schools.

Dissent meant death or the camps. And if ideological submission wasn't enough, there was the endless labour. Citizens were expected to toil for twelve, even fourteen hours a day without rest. The very idea of a holiday, or an eight-hour workday, was ridiculed as bourgeois degeneracy. Even the past was expropriated. In a staggering revision of history, 1967 marked the year North Korea began teaching that it wasn't the Allies who had defeated Imperial Japan, but Kim Il-sung and his guerrilla fighters.

With dissent smothered and the people broken, Kim embarked on one of the most audacious moves in the Communist world—naming a successor. Other socialist states, still pretending to be democracies, kept up the façade. Until the late 1960s, no dictator had dared publicly anoint an heir. The first to shatter the illusion had been Mao Zedong, who chose Lin Biao as his successor in 1969. But the alliance unravelled fast. Rumours swirled of Lin plotting a coup. He fled in 1971—only for his plane to crash in Mongolia, killing everyone on board.

Kim Il-sung had a subtler plan—and a darker one. He selected his own son. It was a move of dynastic brilliance: no son could denounce his father without destroying himself, thought the Great Leader. Kim had three sons: Kim Jong-il,

Kim Phyong-il and Kim Yong-il. It was the eldest, Kim Jong-il, who rose to the top. A flamboyant womaniser with an artistic streak, Jong-il took care to prove his loyalty. He whispered all the right things to all the right officials—many of whom, of course, will have reported back to the father. He even accepted the role of head of Kim Il-sung's personal guard, a not-so-subtle gesture that nothing mattered more than protecting the Great Leader himself.

In February 1974, the succession was official. Kim Jong-il was named heir. No one dared to raise a voice.

It was much later—at the twilight of Kim Il-sung's life, as he began preparing to pass the reins of power to Kim Jong-il—that North Korea lurched into a new age of crises. But the spark that ignited this period of turmoil came not from Pyongyang, but from the seat of its former overlord—Moscow. There, following the 1985 death of the ailing conservative Konstantin Chernenko, Mikhail Gorbachev—the youngest and most reform-minded member of the Politburo—rose to power. What followed soon eclipsed even the boldest predictions: within six years, the Warsaw Pact, the Communist Party of the Soviet Union and the USSR itself would vanish into history.

Across the Communist Bloc, both inside and outside the USSR, hope blossomed. Gorbachev's idealism inspired many. The Kremlin was suddenly hurtling towards reform—censorship relaxed, archives opened, taboos crumbled. Soon it was even permissible to question the very foundations of the regime—to say, out loud, that the Communist Party had no right to rule.

Among those moved by this ideological thaw were a select group of KPA officers studying in Moscow. These weren't dissidents—at least not yet—but handpicked men, each cleared by Kim Jong-il himself to study at the prestigious Frunze Academy. That school's name, and its place in history, carried a sting of irony: Mikhail Frunze, the People's Commissar for Military and Naval Affairs, was rumoured to have been killed by his own Bolshevik comrades. By 1990 the brutalist building would get itself a new neighbour—the South Korean embassy, opened after Seoul and Moscow established diplomatic ties.

Studying in the Soviet Union—by now, that was a novelty for North Korean officers, possibly reminding them of how things used to be decades ago. By the late 1950s, after Pyongyang had begun prising itself free from Moscow's grip, the relationship between the two so-called comrades had turned icy. Officially, both sides still preached 'friendship'— the Soviets didn't want North Korea to tilt fully towards Beijing, and the North still needed Soviet aid. But behind the scenes, it was all frost and friction.

Fast forward to the early 1980s, and the tables had finally begun to turn. Kim Il-sung, alarmed by Deng Xiaoping's China, gingerly reopened lines of communication with the Kremlin. Slowly, relations began to thaw—and a new wave of North Korean students landed in Moscow.

Those who arrived in the late 1980s found themselves in a transformed world. The Soviet Union was liberalising at breakneck speed. Their classrooms were filled with students from Eastern Europe, and the professors no longer recited Marxist dogma with conviction. Communism, for many, was already a relic.

At first, the North Koreans did what they were trained to do: sing the praises of the Great Leader. At cultural exchanges, they'd proudly declare that Kim Il-sung had defeated Imperial Japan and liberated the nation. But instead of applause, they faced scepticism—and, worse, blunt questions.

'Really? Wasn't it the Soviets and the Americans who crushed Japan?'

'You say the Great Leader gives out gifts on his birthday—whose money is he using? His, or the people's?'

'What's his salary?'

'Why is your country ruled by one family—are you still in feudal times?'

With every pointed query, the students' once-unshakeable devotion began to crack. Whispers of doubt spread through the corridors of their dormitories and classrooms, until a far more dangerous current took hold: the whisper of conspiracy. This was perhaps the most serious plot to overthrow the North Korean regime since 1956.

Some of the 1992 plotters are known: Hong Kye-song, later Deputy Chief of Staff; Kang Yong-hwan, Deputy Chief of the Army's Operations Department and a distant relative of Kim Il-sung; and An Jong-ho, Chief of the War Training Department. The officers had seen the Soviet Union transforming before their eyes. They also understood one thing with chilling clarity: no such changes would come to their homeland. Kim Il-sung had no intention of following Gorbachev, nor even China's cautious Deng Xiaoping. And if reform was impossible, only revolution remained.

But how does one reach the Great Leader—a man wrapped in layers upon layers of security, protected by the all-seeing eyes of the state?

The answer, as it turned out, was terrifyingly simple.

There was one moment when Kim Il-sung's location was known, when he would be fully exposed before his army: a military parade. The officers devised a plan so audacious it bordered on madness: load a real shell into one of the tanks set to pass the reviewing stand—and fire. Major-General Kim Il-hun, serving in a tank division of the Pyongyang Defence Command, would have the starring role.

The model was possibly inspired by the assassination of Egypt's Anwar Sadat, killed by Islamist extremists in 1981 at a military parade. The event was widely known in the Soviet Union.

The Kims still suspected nothing. On 23 April 1992, Kim Jong-il promoted Hong Kye-song. Now a Colonel-General, he was the most senior conspirator. In two days, they would strike.

The date chosen for the coup was no accident. It was to be a spectacle, a pageant of power held on 25 April—the day North Korea celebrated the supposed sixtieth anniversary of its military's founding. Kim Il-sung had just turned 80 and had been promoted to Generalissimo, only the second man in the Communist world to hold that archaic title—the first being Stalin himself. Kim Jong-il, for his part, had just donned the uniform of a Marshal of the DPRK. The top brass was decked out with new ranks: Army Minister O Jin-u was now Marshal, eight more became vice-marshals, and over a thousand were elevated to generals.

The entire elite would be there—not only the Kims, but O Jin-u, Vice-Presidents Lee Jong-ok and Pak Song-chol, economic czar Yon Hyong-muk, Foreign Minister Kim Yong-nam, Chief of Staff Choe Gwang, Secretary Kye Ung-thae, eight newly minted Vice-Marshals, and a smattering of foreign dignitaries. The guest list read like a who's who of global autocracy—including Cambodia's King Norodom Sihanouk, Laos' General Secretary Kaysone Phomvihane, and Equatorial Guinea's tyrant Teodoro Obiang Nguema Mbasogo.

But the celebration was founded on a lie. Since 1978, North Korea had claimed that the history of its military stretched back further than it truly did. The Korean People's Army, established in 1948, was now said to be the heir of the Korean People's Revolutionary Army—a mythical guerrilla force allegedly founded by Kim Il-sung himself in 1932.

Later-released Chinese documents suggest that the date in fact marked Kim's enlistment in the Chinese partisan forces in Manchuria—a minor event that North Korean propaganda had inflated into legend.

Still, the state embraced the fiction. The KPA's 'sixtieth birthday' was treated with reverence. In traditional Korean culture, such a birthday, called *hwanggap*, marked the completion of a full zodiac cycle, a time for reflection and renewal. Perhaps ironically, this day could indeed have marked the end of a cycle for the KPA.

And yet fate intervened. A seemingly minor administrative decision derailed the plot. Pak Ki-so, a department chief in the Ministry of the People's Armed Forces, ordered that tanks for the parade should come not from the Pyongyang Defence Command—as the conspirators had planned—but from units directly under the ministry's control. The department chief had no knowledge of the plot, yet his decision saved the regime.

The parade marched on as if nothing was amiss. Tanks thundered down the streets, crowds roared with patriotic fervour, and the grand tribune remained a fortress of untouchability. But behind the scenes, Kim Il-sung and Kim Jong-il were grappling with a chilling truth—they had narrowly escaped complete annihilation.

What followed was nothing short of a reign of terror.

On 8 February 1993, Won Ung-hui, Chief of the KPA Security Department, summoned top officers to a stark hall.

In a cold, unyielding voice, he declared the start of a ruthless purge to 'eliminate traitors'. Names were read aloud, one by one. For each traitor, two grim-faced soldiers of the Security Department moved swiftly: one levelled a gun at the accused, while the other ripped his sacred Kim Il-sung badge and rank insignia from his uniform, handcuffed him, draped a cloak over his shoulders, and dragged him away.

The scene was hauntingly reminiscent of Saddam Hussein's infamous Ba'ath Party purge in 1979—an act designed to strike terror deep into the hearts of the military elite. And, just like in Iraq, the purge was only just beginning.

The Frunze Military Academy had trained officers across all branches, meaning the carnage wasn't confined to tank commanders. The Air Force bore a particularly brutal blow. Skilled pilots—some of the most prized assets of the Korean People's Army—simply vanished without trace. For years afterward, the KPA grappled desperately to fill the void left by these lost aviators.

Meanwhile, Won Ung-hui, the man who had uncovered the conspiracy—and ignited this bloody purge—was handsomely rewarded. Kim Jong-il elevated him from a two-star to a formidable four-star rank, a clear signal of gratitude from a regime shaken to its core.

But what if the Frunze plot had succeeded?

Picture the scene. The tanks roll into Kim Il-sung Square, the crowd roaring, the patriotic anthems blaring from megaphones. Among them is one tank, indistinguishable from the rest, except for the hearts of its crew—pounding like war drums. They know they are seconds away from changing history.

Then, from the tribune, Kim Jong-il—young, sharp-eyed, newly Supreme Commander—notices a turret turning. Something's wrong. This was not rehearsed.

Too late.

The order is given.

'Fire!'

A button is pressed. The primer ignites. A blast of gas hurls the shell from the barrel. Faster than sound, the projectile screams across the square. It strikes the target before anyone there even hears the detonation. In an instant, the tribune vanishes in fire and blood and smoke.

Such a shot wouldn't just have taken the lives of the Kims. The foreign leaders on the tribune would have died too. Cambodia's King Sihanouk's death would have cemented Hun Sen's rule. The Laotian Communist leader Phomvihane's demise would have hastened Khamtai Siphandone's rise. But in Equatorial Guinea the death of Obiang—still President at the time of writing—could have completely changed the country's path.

As for North Korea, with the Great Leader, his heir and the upper crust of the regime obliterated in one deafening instant, it is hard to imagine any path by which the state could have survived. This was not a scenario it had prepared for—not even remotely. But the conspirators had. With the top elite reduced to ash, they could have stepped swiftly into the vacuum, broadcasting to the nation that the tyrant was gone forever.

Perhaps a few diehard loyalists might have dreamed of resistance. But for what? The Great Leader was dead. So was the Supreme Commander. The old order had ceased to exist. There would have been no banner left to rally under, no living symbol of the regime to fight for.

And thus, the new junta would be formed—perhaps called the 'National Salvation Front', to borrow a name from Romania's post-Ceaușescu rebels. What next?

Two scenarios come to mind, though both likely end the same way. First, they could have tried a Gorbachev—reform from within, build 'real' socialism with a human face. Or they could have reached out to Seoul for reunification.

Either way, once a leader is overthrown, no reformer can stop a Communist dictatorship from crumbling. East Germany's Egon Krenz, Bulgaria's Petar Mladenov, Hungary's Károly Grósz were all swept away by history's tide. For Korea, it would have been a tsunami. The dream of unification would have been irresistible—for Northerners yearning for freedom and for Southerners eager to reunite.

If the new Frunze graduate–led junta had asked Seoul for reunification, either right away or following months of chaotic reforms and public agitation, there is little doubt that President Roh Tae-woo would have answered with an enthusiastic yes. Fulfilling the South's stated greatest dream—to bring the Korean people back under one roof—would have been a chance too historic to ignore.

Unifying the two Koreas, so starkly divided in wealth and freedom, would not have been easy. In fact, it would have made the German experience look almost seamless—and, three decades on, Germany still bears the scars of its once-divided past.

But still—it is a haunting thought. That history, in all its crushing weight, might have pivoted on something as banal as a bureaucratic decision about which tank unit would roll through the square. Had the Pyongyang Defence Command kept its place in the parade, had the right turret turned and the right finger pulled the trigger, there might have been no famine, no endless prison camps and no nuclear standoffs.

A unified Korea by the end of 1992.

And all it would have taken was one shell in the right barrel.

10

Bill Clinton's Fire and Fury
The United States could have attacked North Korea in 1993

The North Korean nuclear programme has a long and tangled history. It seems that the very first spark in Kim Il-sung's mind—the first thought to arm his country with a nuclear bomb—came during the Korean War. Back then, General MacArthur toyed with the idea of unleashing a mass atomic strike, hoping to shatter the China–North Korea alliance into submission.

The birthplace of North Korea's nuclear ambitions was the same power that gave the DPRK its existence—the USSR. In the 1950s, Pyongyang sent its brightest physicists to study at Dubna, the beating heart of Soviet nuclear science. Officially, these visits were aimed at building nuclear power plants. But make no mistake: North Korea was quietly eyeing the bomb, waiting for the right moment to claim it.

By 1959, treaties on nuclear assistance had been inked with both China and the Soviet Union. Then, in 1962, the regime established its most notorious nuclear site—the Nyongbyon Nuclear Science Research Centre. Most intelligence on the facility has come via South Korea, which is why the Western world knows it as Yongbyon, its South Korean name. A Soviet reactor was installed there in the 1960s.

The decision to accelerate an active nuclear weapons programme took shape in the 1970s. What sparked this shift remains unclear, though many speculate it was the sudden thaw between the US and China, marked by Nixon and Kissinger's landmark visits to Beijing in 1972—a move that surely rattled Kim Il-sung and sowed deep uncertainty about his regime's security. This looks even more logical given that the détente spurred South Korea to approve its own covert effort to acquire a nuclear arsenal. Seoul only abandoned the programme (codename Plan 890) after pressure and persuasion from Washington.

By the mid-1980s, the North Korean programme was still in its infancy. At the time, Pyongyang leaned closer to the Soviet Union than to China. Moscow, wary of the DPRK's nuclear ambitions, pushed North Korea to join the Treaty on the Non-Proliferation of Nuclear Weapons (NPT). In exchange, the Soviets promised to build a nuclear power plant in the North. Kim Il-sung accepted the deal, and on 12 December 1985, North Korea quietly acceded to the Treaty. Tellingly, the move went unreported in the state press—a sign that the Great Leader saw this as a tactical manoeuvre rather than a strategic shift. In any case, the promised power plant never materialised. When the Soviet Union collapsed, so did any hope of Soviet-built reactors lighting up the North.

Fast-forward to 1992, and Pyongyang was still wearing the mask of a state with zero nuclear aspirations. That year, it signed the Joint Declaration on the Denuclearisation of the Korean Peninsula with South Korea. It also opened its doors—tentatively—to inspections by the International Atomic Energy Agency (IAEA), as required by the NPT. But cracks soon appeared. The IAEA found discrepancies between the declared amount of plutonium and real nuclear waste, raising fears of undeclared stockpiles. Two suspect sites were identified. When inspectors asked to visit them, the mask came off. North Korea said no.

Kim Jong-il, by now Supreme Commander of the KPA, declared a state of prewar readiness. On 12 March 1993, the DPRK announced that it would withdraw from the Treaty. Per NPT rules, the withdrawal would take effect three months later.

Thus began the first of many nuclear standoffs. In Washington, the man at the centre of the storm was President Clinton's Defence Secretary, William Perry. In his memoir, *My Journey at the Nuclear Brink*, Perry admitted that airstrikes on the Yongbyon reactor were considered: 'The strike plan was "on the table," but very far back on the table.' The Americans prioritised diplomacy—for now.

The crisis unfolded in two tense phases. By June 1993, one day before North Korea's withdrawal from the NPT was to become official, Pyongyang agreed to suspend it and permit limited inspections. Talks limped along until April 1994, when the regime once again barred access for IAEA inspectors. Fears mounted that the North was preparing to reprocess spent fuel into weapons-grade plutonium. In May, those fears escalated when North Korea began unloading spent nuclear fuel—a step widely seen as preparation for bomb-making.

The second phase ended not with sabre-rattling, but with a handshake. Enter Jimmy Carter—then the only living Democratic President besides Clinton. In June 1994, Carter flew to Pyongyang and met with Kim Il-sung. To the world's surprise, the talks worked: North Korea offered to suspend reprocessing in exchange for a halt to US sanctions and military escalation. Now Washington had a path forward that did not involve use of force.

After Kim Il-sung's death in July 1994, negotiations resumed. The result was the Agreed Framework, known in Pyongyang as the Geneva Agreement. North Korea would freeze its Yongbyon facilities, halt construction of larger reactors and accept IAEA monitoring. In return, the US—supported by South Korea and Japan—would build two light-water reactors in North Korea and supply heavy fuel oil until those were complete.

For a while, it held. Then came 2002.

BILL CLINTON'S FIRE AND FURY

That year, President George W. Bush branded North Korea part of the 'Axis of Evil'. Assistant Secretary of State James Kelly flew to Pyongyang and accused the North of running a secret uranium enrichment programme. Traces of enriched uranium had reportedly been found on paper taken from Yongbyon—and the US delegation claimed that the North had admitted to it. Pyongyang denied everything.

That moment marked the beginning of the end. Fuel shipments were cut off in December. The following month, North Korea withdrew from the NPT. The Agreed Framework was finished.

So ended the last serious diplomatic attempt to contain the North Korean nuclear programme. All later efforts ended in failure. In 2006, the North conducted its first nuclear test. By the mid-2020s, it had the capacity to strike not just the US West Coast, but perhaps even Washington and New York.

But what if this crisis had not been resolved peacefully? Secretary Perry's memoirs reveal that any war option required authorisation from President Clinton and concurrence from South Korean President Kim Young-sam. This makes military action by the United States highly implausible. One might imagine Clinton—the man who later presided over the bombings of Yugoslavia—giving the green light, but for President Kim, this would have been far less likely. After all, following the Korean War, Seoul was effectively hostage to the North—the capital lay well within range of North Korean artillery, and any aggressive move risked devastating the city.

But let us imagine something extraordinary. Negotiations fail at round one and Kim Young-sam becomes convinced that North Korea is indeed on the verge of producing a nuclear bomb. Perhaps he fears that the ailing Kim Il-sung will see this weapon as his last chance to reinvade the South while still alive. After President Clinton presents the military option, Kim Young-sam grudgingly agrees. OpPlan 5027, the long-standing war plan to repel a North Korean invasion, is revised, and the operation to strike Yongbyon is authorised. In the dead of night, a USAF bomber wing takes off from South Korean or Japanese soil, penetrates North Korean airspace and unleashes a devastating barrage, reducing the facility to rubble.

What would have happened next? No one can say for sure, but the consequences could have been catastrophic. These were the final months of Kim Il-sung's rule. With Yongbyon destroyed, the Great Leader might well have authorised a furious retaliatory strike—driven by rage or a desperate refusal to appear weak.

Events in 2010—the North Korean sinking of a South Korean corvette and the shelling of an island in the Yellow Sea—have shown that even a few dozen deaths can be enough to turn South Korean public opinion decisively against the North. A major retaliatory strike in 1993 could have unleashed full-scale war—the very conflict a military operation would have sought to avoid. With no nuclear weapons, a collapsing economy, broken ties with China, a largely pro-Western Russia and the Supreme Leader nearing the end of his life, such a war might indeed have ended North Korea, but at an enormous human cost: countless lives lost, cities razed. And, with Seoul bombarded, the South Korean economy would have suffered a crippling blow, making any prospect of reintegrating the North a far more arduous endeavour.

Of all the counterfactuals explored in this book, this one stands out not only as one of the least likely, but also one of the deadliest. In that grim alternate history, freedom would have been bought at a truly terrible price.

11

Crash Landing

In 1994, Kim Jong-il could have boarded the medical helicopter flying to save Kim Il-sung

North Korea has never revealed where Kim Il-sung died.

On 9 July 1994, at noon, a solemn news anchor delivered the stunning announcement of the Great Leader's demise. *Rodong Sinmun* published a medical bulletin: myocardial infarction—or, more plainly, a heart attack. Kim's embalmed body was soon laid out in state in his own palace, now rebranded as a mausoleum.

But where had he actually died?

South Korean outlets swiftly triangulated the likely location: Kim's villa in the Myohyang mountains. That night, three helicopters had departed Pyongyang, braving an almost biblical downpour to reach the villa. Meanwhile, US military intelligence intercepted a stark message from the site: 'The doctors are not here yet.' Later testimony has filled in the grim details—Kim Il-sung felt sick, doctors were dispatched, two helicopters crashed in the storm and, with no aid on hand, the man who ruled North Korea for nearly half a century died.

One overlooked detail emerges from those accounts: the helicopters were meant to carry one more passenger. Kim Jong-il had insisted on flying to his father's side, and only relentless pleading from his wife, Ko Yong-hui, and his guards had kept him from boarding.

Here the mind cannot help but wander. What if he had ignored them? For decades, Kim Jong-il played the role of loyalist-in-chief—and what purer expression of loyalty than to defy a monsoon to be at the Great Leader's side in his final hour? But we now know such a gesture could have killed him. And with that, history may have pivoted sharply off its axis.

Imagine, for a moment, the paralysing terror that would have seized the North Korean elite had both the Great Leader and the Dear Leader perished that night. The 1990s were already an age of crumbling certainties—Eastern Europe had unravelled, the Soviet Union collapsed, Mongolia turned to democracy, and China's bloody stand at Tiananmen was still fresh in memory. Beijing had just recognised Seoul, severing what little warmth remained with Pyongyang. The North Korean economy, gutted by chronic mismanagement and the sudden withdrawal of foreign aid, was in freefall. The country had been told for twenty years that Kim Il-sung's death would herald Kim Jong-il's rise—but no one planned for both men to vanish at once.

Curiously, the matter of succession was not entirely opaque. There was, after all, a clear number three: Marshal O Jin-u. As Minister of the People's Armed Forces, Chief of Staff of the Korean People's Army and First Vice-Chairman of the National Defence Commission, Marshal O was the highest-ranking military figure in the land. His 1985 elevation to Vice-Marshal—the first such promotion in over three decades—signalled that he was not just another general. In a surreal propaganda stunt in 1986, North Korean loudspeakers at the DMZ had announced for three days that 'Kim Il-sung had died'—probably because Kim was curious about what might happen when he actually did. Among the conflicting narratives the KPA was feeding to the South during these days was the claim that 'O Jin-u has taken power and the people support him.'

So, yes, in this alternate timeline, the elite could have rallied. Marshal O might have been swiftly installed as President and General Secretary. Speeches would be delivered, tears shed, statues wreathed and vows of eternal loyalty repeated. But after that? The future would be far murkier.

Marshal O lacked the mythos. He was not part of the sacred bloodline. No cult swirled around his name. His status rested solely on his proximity to Kim Il-sung and his battlefield credentials as a loyal partisan. There was no mythic aura of genius, no 'Sun of the Twenty-First Century' narrative to prop him up.

And he was old. In July 1994, O was 78. He died just seven months after the helicopter crash. He might not even have lasted that long, if he'd been saddled with the weight of the nation and the trauma of dual bereavement.

O would have inherited not just a nation, but a crisis. The simultaneous deaths of father and son would have emboldened every dormant dissident, from the reformist official in the Central Committee, to the jaded General, the sceptical Colonel, the restless student. In reality, Kim Jong-il's seamless succession drained the air from the room. It closed the door on the possibility of change. But Marshal O would not have had that privilege. This was the moment when North Korea might have followed Albania's path.

Albania, an isolated Stalinist enclave in the Balkans, closely mirrored North Korea for decades. Its leader, Enver Hoxha, had denounced first Tito's Yugoslavia, then Khrushchev's USSR, then Mao's China—all for betraying Stalin. For years, the terror of the *Sigurimi*, the Albanian secret police, crushed any hope.

But then Hoxha died. His successor, Ramiz Alia, a loyalist, inherited a crumbling system amid a crushing economic crisis. Protests began quietly in the countryside; then workers joined students. Demands for reform evolved into calls to dismantle the regime. In February 1991, the people tore down Hoxha's statue in Tirana's Skanderbeg Square and beat back the *Sigurimi* who tried to stop them. The spell broke. The Politburo, paralysed by fear of retribution, capitulated. The Albanian dictatorship collapsed.

North Korea, too, had a statue.

A towering bronze of Kim Il-sung unveiled in 1972, to mark his sixtieth birthday, glowers over Pyongyang from Mansu Hill. One cannot help but wonder: if Kim Jong-il had flown that night and died in the storm, would that statue also have fallen? Would it have heralded a new age—not just of rubble and reckoning, but of rebirth?

12

The Soldiers' Revolution
The Sixth Corps' rebellion of 1995 could have succeeded

Kim Il-sung was dead. For the first time in the history of the Democratic People's Republic of Korea, power passed from one pair of hands to another. But, as Kim Jong-il slipped into his father's shoes, the ground beneath him was already buckling.

The economy had collapsed in all but name. Hunger gnawed at the fringes of the nation, heralding a famine that would claim hundreds of thousands of lives—perhaps even more. In the northern city of Chongjin, amid the cold and the hunger, a plot was born. Bold, desperate, and swiftly snuffed out, it has since drifted into near-legend. At its heart was the Sixth Corps of the Korean People's Army.

What happened remains one of the many unsolved riddles that litter North Korea's history. Though testimonies are rare and much remains sealed away, enough has trickled through the cracks for us to sketch at least a likely chain of events—and it reads like the plot of a Cold War thriller.

Paranoia is the regime's native tongue. Its military is riddled with internal checks designed to keep commanders from acting on their own. A typical order requires not one signature, but three: the commander, the political officer (in charge of ideology and Party affairs) and the security officer—North Korea's version of the military police.

One might imagine that this system exists to let the political and security officers sniff out disloyalty among commanders. But the story of the Sixth Corps turns that logic on its head. It was the Commissar—the political officer, the one meant to be most fanatically loyal—who cracked first. After watching the country slip into starvation and ruin, he dared to ask what no one else would: what if the problem wasn't the Americans, or saboteurs, or corrupt local officials? What if the rot began at the top?

And then, astonishingly, he acted. This Lieutenant-General, disgusted and disillusioned, began recruiting fellow officers. The Corps' own security chief joined him. Together, they imagined something unthinkable: the fall of the Kim dynasty.

With two of the three key figures on board, they approached the final piece—the Corps commander. If he joined, they could seize Chongjin, declare their defection to the world, reach out to South Korea's military, and begin the long march to Pyongyang.

But the plan never left the ground. The commander, the one man whose approval they needed most, refused. In a cruel twist, this career soldier proved more loyal than the Commissar or the security chief, putting to rest any romantic illusions about professional soldiers being more independent than their so-called minders.

His reward? Death. The commander was murdered—a bloody overture to what might have become civil war.

But Kim Jong-il had a nose for betrayal. He had caught wind of the conspiracy early and responded with trademark brutality. He dispatched Kim Yong-chun, a rising star in the military, to snuff out the flames. And he did just that.

He didn't wait for intelligence reports or thorough investigations. General Kim acted immediately. The conspirators were arrested en masse. The purge that followed was swift and ruthless. The would-be revolutionaries were executed, and the Sixth Corps was erased—disbanded, deleted from the military's order of battle as though it had never existed. Troops from across the nation poured into Chongjin, sealing the city under a blanket of fear.

Whispers still claim that every officer above company commander was put to death. Unproven, yes—but even loyalists believe it. Today, the Korean People's Army has no 'Corps No. 6'. It was airbrushed out of existence, like a disgraced official scrubbed from an old propaganda poster.

But, for a brief, flickering moment in 1995, the regime stared into the abyss. The threat wasn't foreign sanctions or global condemnation. It was mutiny. The coup failed, but its echo remains—a chilling reminder that, even in the most suffocating dictatorship, loyalty is never absolute. And history, sometimes, almost turns.

The tale of the Sixth Corps raised more questions than answers—so many, in fact, that some South Koreans began to doubt whether it had ever happened at all. Could it really have been a mutiny? Or was it, as some Pyongyang watchers whispered, nothing more than a convenient power struggle? Perhaps Kim Yong-chun had simply harboured a grudge against the Corps' Commissar, and done away with him the old-fashioned way—by branding him a traitor.

There's no way to know for certain. But one thing points strongly to the conspiracy being real: Pyongyang's reaction.

Had this been an ordinary purge—a personal vendetta, or even a bout of political paranoia—the regime would likely have followed the usual grim routine. The accused would be tortured and executed, their families exiled to the camps. That was standard fare under Kim Il-sung and, while somewhat softened under Kim Jong-il, the machinery remained in place. But dismantling an entire Corps? Stripping it from the KPA's structure, leaving a conspicuous void in the numbering system? That was unprecedented. And it hasn't happened since.

Then there's the fate of Kim Yong-chun himself. For his role in the purge, he wasn't just rewarded—he was catapulted skyward. First to Vice-Marshal, then to Marshal of the

Korean People's Army. It's the highest military rank anyone besides the Supreme Commander can hold.

Titles in North Korea are never handed out lightly. This was a promotion soaked in blood and secrecy—a clear signal that Kim Yong-chun had done something extraordinary. All signs point to a coup that wasn't just imagined, but attempted. And for a brief, terrifying heartbeat, it came close enough to shake the foundations of a regime built on absolute control.

So, let's imagine. What if the plot had worked? What if the Sixth Corps had had a different commander—one willing to roll the dice, to join the coup?

We know almost nothing about the inner workings of the conspiracy. Did the plan call for seizing local communications first? The Chongjin Party Committee? The regional headquarters of the Department for Protection of State Security—the feared political police? We can only guess. But even a partially successful first strike could have set events spiralling beyond control.

Pyongyang's gut reaction would almost certainly have been to isolate the rebellious city—lock it down, seal it off, smother the story before the outside world caught wind. But Chongjin had a unique wrinkle. It was the only city in North Korea, besides the capital, to host a permanent foreign diplomatic presence. The Chinese and Russian consulates were right there, staffed by seasoned envoys—Zhang Yuanwei and Aleksandr Putivets. Both would have had access to secure communication systems. Both would almost certainly have sent word to their capitals.

And once Moscow and Beijing knew, so would the rest of the world.

Suddenly, you've got a recipe for civil war—one drenched in blood, because for both sides, defeat meant certain death. The outcome would have been impossible to predict. Would Bill Clinton and President Kim Young-sam have intervened? Would Jiang Zemin have backed Pyongyang—or quietly stepped aside? And what of Boris Yeltsin? Would he have helped topple the North Korean regime, or stood back and watched it burn?

We'll never know. But one thing is certain: had the rebellion succeeded, the cost would have been staggering. And yet—perhaps—it would have been worth it. Kim Jong-il's reign might have been cut short. The famine, which would go on to claim so many lives, might have been averted. And 20 million people—along with generations yet unborn—might have been handed a fragile but priceless thing: the chance of a better tomorrow.

PART IV

CRACKS IN THE DYNASTY

2000s–20s

13

One-Way Train

The explosion at Ryongchon Station could have claimed the life of Kim Jong-il

For more than a decade after the dissolution of the Sixth Corps, Kim Jong-il's grip on power remained unshaken. The catastrophic famine of the 1990s, by even the most conservative estimates, claimed hundreds of thousands of lives. Kim's response was defiant resistance to any calls for real change. In 1999, he famously declared: 'We must never be dragged along by the clamour of the imperialists for "reform" and "opening up". "Reform" and "opening up" are the road to national ruin. We cannot allow even the slightest bit of "reform" or "opening up".'

Meanwhile, people were fleeing to China, gambling that a desperate dash across the border was still better than starving slowly at home. This was where the cracks began to show. The state lost its grip on large parts of the economy. Food rations stopped, and makeshift marketplaces sprang up across the country. People started trading, bartering and otherwise surviving outside the decaying framework of the state.

Then came a turning point. In 2001, Kim Jong-il visited China and was stunned by what he saw: glittering cities, bustling markets, the rewards of reform. Something shifted. Back home, he eased up ever so slightly. The regime quietly stopped cracking down on those 'unsocialist' markets. But the reforms were narrow and half-hearted. Price controls stayed in place; private property remained unrecognised; and, politically, Kim gave up nothing.

And yet, for all his iron rule, the 2000s brought moments when it could have ended. The first came on 22 April 2004. Kim Jong-il was returning from China by train—the infamous Sun Train, his heavily armoured rolling fortress. Anyone tracking his movements would've known the route. After Sinuiju Chongynon and Sinuiju South, the next stop was Ryongchon. He was vulnerable on that day.

Then it happened. At ten minutes past noon, a colossal explosion tore through Ryongchon Station.

The blast obliterated the station and shredded the nearby railway. Houses in the vicinity collapsed. Roofs vanished, walls crumbled. Worst of all, Ryongchon's primary school was nearby. Children were among the dead.

Over a hundred people perished. More than a thousand were wounded. Thousands more lost their homes or livelihoods. Foreign governments offered help; Pyongyang accepted medical supplies, but barred foreign doctors from the site.

The regime rushed to spin the tragedy into a tale of loyalty and heroism—one that looked very chilling, when you understood that true virtue lied in prioritising the Leader's picture over the lives of children. State media reported:

> During a lesson at Ryongchon Primary School, a powerful explosion caused the building to collapse and set the classrooms on fire. In the midst of it, 32-year-old teacher Han Un-suk first moved the portraits of President **Kim Il-sung** and Comrade **Kim Jong-il** to safety. She then rescued seven students before sacrificing her life. Another teacher, Han Jong-suk, also perished, holding the portraits in her hands.

For the regime, the most terrifying thing wasn't the casualties. It wasn't even the sacred portraits. It was the timing. That explosion, had it gone off moments later or slightly nearer, could have annihilated the Sun Train.

What had caused it? Theories swirled. North Korea's official version blamed a collision involving a train carrying ammonium nitrate fertiliser. Others said a spark from a power line had ignited explosives. Some blamed volatile cargo: oil, liquid gas. And then there was the darker rumour—that it was no accident at all.

According to leaked diplomatic cables from Wikileaks, Kim Jong-il believed it was an assassination attempt, triggered by a mobile phone. Paranoid? Maybe. But paranoia didn't mean they weren't out to get him. In the aftermath, mobile phones were banned for several years.

And here's the thing: the Sun Train doesn't stand out. To the untrained eye, it looks just like any other North Korean train. It's entirely plausible that someone had tried to kill the Great Commander—and got the wrong target.

What if they had succeeded?

Imagine this: Kim Jong-il has left China just a few hours earlier—and then, at Ryongchon Station, the Sun Train goes nova.

The blast wouldn't only have killed Kim Jong-il, his guards and the train staff. Travelling with him were other key figures of the regime—Prime Minister Pak Pong-ju, his fellow reformist Yon Hyong-muk, and the seasoned diplomat Kang Sok-chu. All gone in a flash. Most crucially, Vice-Marshal Kim Yong-chun, the man who had crushed the Sixth Corps rebellion in the '90s, would have perished. He wouldn't have been around for the power struggle to come.

And there would indeed have been a struggle. The burning question: who takes over? Who's strong enough to hold together the crumbling edifice of the regime? In 2004, Kim Jong-il hadn't yet named a successor.

None of his sons was a serious contender. The eldest, Kim Jong-nam, was living in effective exile and hadn't set foot in North Korea for years. The second, Kim Jong-chol, preferred guitars to guns. The youngest, Kim Jong-un, just 20 at the time, was utterly unknown to the elite—no experience, no clout.

Another ambitious relative, Jang Song-thaek, Kim's brother-in-law, was also out of the picture. By early 2004, he'd been purged—disgraced for a mix of womanising, corruption and political infighting with Prime Minister Pak, then Kim's favourite. In short, a family succession looked dead in the water.

The real danger was that North Korea lacked not only a succession plan, but an emergency plan. Despite all its rituals and slogans, there was no protocol for what should happen if the Supreme Leader suddenly ceased to be. Formally, the Party was meant to rule—its Politburo and Presidium making the big calls. But Kim Jong-il had mothballed that system. Since his father's death, no Politburo plena had been held. Even Kim's own rise to General Secretary in 1997 had happened by acclamation, not through any formal Party process.

By the time of the train disaster in April 2004, the Politburo was a hollow shell. Many members had simply died of old age. Kim Jong-il stood alone in the Presidium. Of the six full members left, three were Secretaries—Han Song-ryong, Chon Byong ho and Kye Ung-thae (the latter reportedly in cognitive decline)—while the rest were elderly placeholders: Kim Yong-nam of the Foreign Policy

Department, Kim Yong-ju (Kim Il-sung's brother, aged 83), and 90-year-old Pak Song-chol, a former prime minister.

In that vacuum, power would almost certainly have passed to the one institution Kim truly trusted—the National Defence Commission. Once obscure, Kim had elevated it as the regime's real centre of gravity. He chaired it himself, with Jo Myong-rok—head of the Army's General Political Bureau—as First Deputy Chairman. Other members included Armed Forces Minister Kim Il-chol, Vice-Marshal Lee Yong-mu, General O Kuk-ryol, and Second Economy Committee Chair Paek Se-bong. Chon Byong-ho also sat on the NDC. But two key members—Kim Yong-chun and Yon Hyong-muk—would have died on the train.

Which leaves one obvious successor: promote the number two to number one. Jo Myong-rok.

If any figure could have been presented to the public as a plausible Supreme Leader in 2004, it would have been Jo. That's what deputies are for—to step in when the boss can't.

But Jo was no politician. He was a soldier—a Korean War veteran, a pilot, a product of military hierarchy. In the 1950s, as North Korea scrambled to train jet pilots, Jo Myong-rok had been sent to the USSR. The Air Force became his life. In 1980, he rose to command it, staying in post for eighteen years. He was widely credited with keeping the Air Force afloat after the Frunze purge gutted its ranks in 1995. That year, he rose even higher, becoming head of the Army's ideological watchdog, the General Political Bureau. Three years later, Kim made him his top deputy at the National Defence Commission.

Those who dealt with Jo—both subordinates in the Air Force and Americans who met him during his surreal 2000 trip to the White House—described a quiet, rule-bound man, cautious and loyal to Kim Jong-il. Fearful of him, even.

So, had he been handed the keys to the kingdom in 2004, what would he have done?

Frankly, it's almost impossible to say. A North Korea under Jo Myong-rok would have faced enormous challenges. The elite's expectations were sky-high—and not out of idealism. They wanted survival. No one was keen to be executed or sent to prison if the system imploded.

Let's glance at the dilemmas Chairman Jo would have had to tackle—without pretending that we can know how he would have answered them.

Should North Korea embark on real economic reform? Should the iron grip of state terror be loosened—or should a new wave of purges hammer home who was now in charge? What of the sacred cult of Kim Il-sung and Kim Jong-il—preserve it, scale it back, or dismantle it entirely in favour of glorifying the new boss? Was Jo even ready to do what Khrushchev had done in Moscow—and denounce the dead tyrant?

Then there's the nuclear question. In 2004, North Korea was edging closer to the bomb. The first test would come in

2006. Should Jo have pushed ahead—or called it off and tried cutting a deal with the George W. Bush administration?

Should the doors to the South be nudged further open, or slammed shut before dangerous ideas slipped through? And what about China? Was it time to lean on Beijing—to offer loyalty to Jiang Zemin's successor, Hu Jintao, in return for backing?

So many questions. So few answers.

But one thing is certain: the Ryongchon explosion could have derailed not just the Pyongyang–Sinuiju railway, but the course of history itself.

14

End of the Line
Kim Jong-il's 2008 stroke could have proved lethal

Four years after his narrow brush with death at Ryongchon, August 2008 saw Marshal Kim Jong-il in a flurry of activity. The Supreme Commander traversed the country with trademark vigour, inspecting military units as the state press breathlessly recorded his every move. From bedrooms to barracks, pig farms to food stores, he dispensed his 'august instructions' like divine mandates, determined to improve the lives of his soldiers. No sign of catastrophe lingered in the air—until 15 August. Then, disaster struck.

Kim Jong-il had a stroke.

It wasn't entirely surprising. The Great Commander was never known for moderation. He drank heavily and favoured fine cognac; at 67, his lifestyle was catching up with him. Yet, with the nation's top doctors at his beck and call, few had expected such a dramatic collapse. As he slipped into a coma, the elite plunged into chaos.

Faced with a medical emergency the regime could not handle alone, Pyongyang reached out—to France. A quiet call was made to neurosurgeon François-Xavier Roux, requesting his presence in North Korea to treat a critically important patient. Only upon arrival did Professor Roux discover who lay waiting on the operating table—Kim Jong-il himself. But it wasn't their first meeting: the two had crossed paths fifteen years earlier, after Kim fell from a horse in 1993 and suffered a cerebral contusion.

This time, the stakes were much higher. The Great Marshal lay unconscious. The state hung in the balance.

Against the odds, Dr Roux pulled Kim back from the brink. But the leader would remain absent from public view for nearly two months. Not until 11 October did North Koreans see his face again in state media—a carefully staged reappearance designed to show strength.

But what if he had never come back?

In August 2008, North Korea was still woefully unprepared for a sudden succession. Kim had learned little from the train explosion. Since 2004, the top configuration had shifted slightly—Politburo elders Kye Ung-thae and Yon Hyong-muk had passed away, while First Deputy Chairman Jo Myong-rok was increasingly frail with age. The Politburo remained dormant. The National Defence Commission (NDC), by default, was seen as the country's true seat of power.

Foreign analysts were already anticipating Kim's death, their speculation swirling around familiar names: one of his three sons, or perhaps his brother-in-law, Jang Song-thaek, the shadowy operator married to Kim Kyong-hui. With hindsight, two guesses were clearly off. Kim Jong-nam, the eldest, had fallen out of favour. Kim Jong-chol, the second, showed no appetite for power. That left two: Jang and Kim Jong-un.

But neither man was ready.

Had Kim died that August, neither Jong-un nor Jang would have had the political muscle to grab the throne. Jang, only recently returned from exile, was still a mid-tier Party functionary. Jong-un, more strikingly, held no official post at all. Neither sat on the Politburo or the NDC. In the event of an emergency conclave, both would likely have been excluded—and discarded, much like Vasiliy Stalin. The son of the Soviet tyrant, once a rising star, was swiftly sidelined after his father's death, dying in obscurity a decade later. So, who would have taken over?

Jo Myong-rok? Perhaps—but not likely by this time. At 80, Jo had little time left. He died in 2010. And, in this version of events, he faced a far more formidable rival. Enter Kim Yong-chun, the Sixth Corps' executioner.

The Deputy Chairman of the NDC, Kim Yong-chun had a powerful hand, and the ambition to match. Had Kim Jong-il died in 2004 aboard the Sun Train, Kim Yong-chun, travelling with him, would've died too. But in 2008, he was not only alive—he was rising.

One sign stood out. On 9 September, North Korea's national day, with Kim Jong-il still incapacitated, it was Kim Yong-chun who stepped forward to deliver the regime's formal address. That speech may well have been a signal. In many Communist states, the man asked to chair key events in the leader's absence often became the successor.

Yong-chun had the credentials. As the man who crushed the Sixth Corps' coup attempt, he had shown himself capable in moments of peril—precisely the kind of resolve the Party would need after Kim's death. His decisive reputation could have been weaponised for propaganda. One can almost hear *Rodong Sinmun* proclaim:

> In the dark days of the Arduous March, when traitors schemed against the Republic, comrade **Kim Yong-chun**, the most loyal of loyal followers of the Great Commander, smashed their wicked machinations with exemplary bravery, in true Songun spirit. The National Defence Commission of the Democratic People's Republic of Korea addressed the Supreme People's Assembly, nominating Comrade **Kim Yong-chun** to be elected its Chairman. Today, he stands at the helm of our revolution.

Had the handover taken that path, North Korea might have swerved in a wholly different direction.

And it seems that Kim Jong-il understood that.

Following his recovery, the Great Commander moved with urgency. His medical scans, sent to Dr Roux in France, had been intercepted by US and South Korean intelligence, who concluded he had just three to five years left to live. Kim likely knew this too.

And so, on 8 January 2009—Kim Jong-un's 25th birthday—he summoned Organisation and Guidance Department chief Lee Je-gang. Jong-un, he announced, would be his successor.

Over the next year, the regime shifted gears. A rare Party conference named Kim Jong-un as Deputy Chairman of the Central Military Commission, and installed a fresh cohort of cadres across Party institutions.

Though Kim Jong-il would die just two years later in 2011, he had ensured that the path was clear. The dynastic succession continued, and the third generation of Kim family rule began—not with a coup or a scramble, but with calculated design.

15

Broken Bonds

Unrest following the failed currency reform of 2009 could have led to a general uprising

Kim Jong-un was named successor in January 2009. It did not take long for the international press to catch wind of what was unfolding in Pyongyang: North Korea was preparing for a third-generation dynastic succession—an extraordinary development for a regime that strenuously denies it is a monarchy. According to some reports, the 25-year-old heir apparent was placed in charge of the country's secret police. Official propaganda soon dubbed him the 'Young General', and he appeared to take a keen interest in military affairs.

Yet the final crisis of the Kim Jong-il era had little to do with his designated successor. Its roots were economic.

Throughout the 2000s, North Korea's economic direction was shaped by an internal rivalry between two camps: moderate reformists, led by Pak Pong-ju—a former factory director and later Minister of Chemical Industry—and conservative hardliners, whose de facto leader, Pak Nam-gi, had held senior posts in the State Planning Committee since the mid-1970s. Policy shifts often depended on which faction held Kim Jong-il's ear.

After a landmark trip to China in 2001, during which Kim was reportedly awestruck by that country's economic transformation, the reformists gained ground. In 2002–3, North Korea adjusted state prices to better reflect market realities, initiated economic co-operation with South Korea, and ceased the persecution of grassroots market traders who had emerged in the aftermath of the Great Famine. At one point, Kim even entertained the notion of turning the border city of Sinuiju into a kind of North Korean Macau—a Special Administrative Region with minimal state control and open access for outsiders. The scheme collapsed, however, when China arrested the man appointed to govern it, Yang Bin, signalling its strong disapproval of Pyongyang seeking to establish such an autonomous enclave without having consultated Beijing.

Pak Pong-ju was nonetheless elevated to Prime Minister, becoming the regime's top economic official.

But as time passed, Kim's favour began shifting back towards the conservatives. Perhaps it was the Ryongchon train explosion, which Kim reportedly interpreted as an assassination attempt. The aftermath saw a nationwide ban on mobile phones, lasting several years. Or perhaps it was simply palace intrigue—well-timed whispers and well-placed flattery. Whatever the cause, by the mid-2000s, reform had been stalled. In 2007, Pak Pong-ju was unceremoniously dismissed and replaced by his own Transport Minister. Kim increasingly brought Pak Nam-gi with him on inspection tours, signalling a realignment of loyalties. Around 2005, Pak was appointed head of the Party's Planning and Finance Department.

It was under Pak Nam-gi's direction that the country plunged into a wholly avoidable crisis. To anyone with a basic grasp of economics, the plan was farcical. But Pak, whose background lay in the rigid orthodoxy of the State Planning Committee, seemed oblivious to the realities of even rudimentary fiscal policy.

His scheme was bold in its folly. Backed by Kim Jong-il, he launched a currency revaluation: 100 old won would now equal 1 new won. But the true calamity lay in what he chose to do with wages. Rather than reducing salaries accordingly, he left them untouched. Prices were to fall by a factor of 100, yet incomes would remain the same. It appears that Pak Nam-gi genuinely believed this would make everyone rich—an almost childlike misreading of economic fundamentals.

The policy was a strange mix of careful planning and spectacular blundering. Small banknotes for the new won had been printed as far back as 2002—so even the reformists had been thinking ahead about this, probably dreaming of a calmer, more sensible reset than the one the conservatives ironically oversaw. The big bills only appeared in 2008, right after the conservatives had clawed their way back into Kim Jong-il's good graces.

Then chaos took over.

The government announced the reform on 30 November 2009. But not on the TV or radio—those outlets were forbidden to mention it. Instead, news was brought to the public through internal channels. The first rule was harsh: people could only exchange up to 100,000 won—a pitiful US$26 on the black market. For traders who had stashed away their life's savings, this was a nightmare. Their money was about to turn into dust.

The state demanded people hand over their savings, promising to pay up the next day.

But on 1 December, confusion exploded. Three different orders came down, twisting the rules like a rollercoaster. First, the limit jumped to 150,000 won in cash and 300,000 in bank accounts. Then it slammed back to 100,000, with any money over that confiscated at an insane 1,000:1 rate—effectively stealing 90 per cent of savings above the cutoff. Then came a final kick: only those with more than 100,000 won in bank accounts could exchange anything. The savings above the limit weren't repaid in cash, but in certificates with a vague promise of repayment.

Students got the worst deal—only allowed to swap 30,000 won. The rest of their money? Gone.

Rules kept shifting—by 3 December, the limit was 100,000 won, plus 50,000 per household member. That was the fifth set of instructions in just four days.

The country boiled over.

Prices shot up, as salaries, in theory, had jumped by a hundredfold overnight. And the clock was ticking: come 6 December, the old won would be worthless. But the government wasn't easing off. It cracked down hard on vendor markets—those vital hubs of survival—calling them dens of 'unsocialist activities'. On 11 December, the regime banned food sales in markets, trying to force a return to the state's stranglehold.

The rich were caught in a dire situation. Desperate, they struck deals with poorer folk, who would register the money as their own in return for a 30 per cent cut. Some of the elite even burned their money, thinking that submitting it to the state for an exchange could lead to questions about the wealth's origins. The state quickly outlawed this desperate move, threatening persecution for money-burning.

With markets disrupted, people struggled to buy basics. Fearful of what was coming, many abandoned work to rush to the shops, spending their dwindling savings as city loudspeakers blasted fresh, baffling rules.

Foreign currency–holders were a rare group feeling somewhat safe—until the government cracked down on them, too. Suddenly, foreign cash was illegal in Pyongyang. Panic selling flooded the market, with sellers taking massive losses and receiving rapidly devaluing won. Others bought scarce home appliances, draining supplies. In the capital, the state temporarily shut down the phone network to stop rumours and unrest from spreading.

Shock and anger gripped the nation. As winter approached, savings vanished overnight. A man from Sinuiju near China said it best: 'Everything goes blurry before my eyes, and all the strength drains from my hands.' For some, the stress proved to be deadly, as for a woman trader in Sunchon who'd just landed a 90 million-won deal, only to see nearly all of it vanish. She died of a heart attack.

People began to question the state's rosy promises. 'They said it'd be a year of turnover,' one trader said bitterly. 'Now I see what kind of turnover they meant.'

Meanwhile, the Party told cadres to push the reform as a socialist victory. But who would believed that? What use was a 'strong, prosperous nation' tomorrow when you couldn't eat today?

Even the officials grew doubtful. At regional meetings, lower-level cadres demanded real action as people's lives fell apart. The Central Committee ordered feedback—and it was overwhelmingly negative. By January 2010, some cadres were warning: things might just spiral out of control.

Then came the flu.

A wave of influenza had struck in December, adding to the misery. Stressed, malnourished and furious, people were defenceless. The regime tried to bury the news—politically inconvenient—but, in another sense, the outbreak was strangely welcome. Sick citizens don't protest. And now the government had an excuse to clamp down on movement. The outbreak was declared a 'Grade 11 emergency'—a level once reserved for wounded Korean War soldiers.

In January, the regime tried to buy loyalty with payouts to workers and farmers. People took their money straight to markets. Pyongyang didn't like that one bit. It moved to shut down Phyongsong Market, the biggest outside the capital, and Sunam Market in Chongjin. The plan was to demolish the latter and build apartments. But both survived—too vital to their cities' economies to destroy.

By February, it had become evident to the top leadership that the entire scheme had been a disaster, and someone had to be held accountable. The target was clear: Pak Nam-gi. Kim Jong-il branded him a 'spy who had infiltrated the ranks of the revolution'. Arrested by State Security, Pak was subjected to a relentless barrage of accusations. It was claimed that, during the Korean War, he had been a member of a right-wing militia; and that, in the 1950s, he had allied himself with Choe Chang-ik and his factionalists. They even forced a 'confession' from him, alleging that Pak had sought to radically marketise the North Korean economy in a bid to undermine Party control—effectively painting this archconservative as a radical liberal. The verdict was clear and preordained: death.

Then, on 10 March, the Ministry of the People's Armed Forces rounded up dozens of North Korean officials, of Vice-Minister rank and above, and took them to the Kang Kon Military Academy in Pyongyang. Many must have known what was coming: it was the regime's favourite execution site, the spot where the leadership preferred to carry out killings in front of the elite, but hidden from the public eye.

Pak Nam-gi, beaten and bound by State Security, was among them. Nine shots rang out; it's likely he was killed by the first one, which struck his head.

Afterward, it's said, Kim Jong-un ordered Pak's body to be tossed into a metal furnace and incinerated. The appointed successor, who had initially shown some support for the currency reform, now wanted to shift the blame squarely onto Pak Nam-gi. The state made every effort to convince the public that the entire disastrous scheme had been Pak's brainchild and that he alone was responsible.

With Pak Nam-gi's death, Kim Jong-il's favour swung back to the reformist bloc. They stabilised the economy, and this direction endured for a few years, even after Kim's death in 2011.

Unlike many earlier crises of the Kim Jong-il era, this one was not driven by a quirk of fate or a rebellious army, but by ordinary citizens. We know from interviews with escapees, and rare comments shared quietly from within the country, that North Koreans still recall December 2009 as the month they were truly, viscerally angry.

What if that anger had boiled over? A slight shift, a single spark, and the regime might have lost its grip. Reports from that tense winter speak of officials who feared exactly that.

History has seen how a misjudged descent into monetary chaos can unravel a dictatorship. In Burma, General Ne Win's bizarre reforms—voiding banknotes he deemed 'unlucky', like 25 and 75 kyat—helped trigger the 1988 uprising that ultimately forced him to step down.

Then there was Tunisia. Less than a year after North Korea's own monetary disaster, in late 2010, street vendor Mohamed Bouazizi, manhandled and humiliated by police, set himself alight. His final act sparked the Arab Spring, bringing down governments across the Middle East and plunging Libya, Yemen and Syria into years of bloodshed.

North Korea, too, stood at a cliff's edge. A ruined trader might have taken their own life. A crowd could have gathered. Shots might have rung out. What if, just once, a security officer refused the order to fire? The machinery of repression could have jammed. Would the regime have scrambled to recover, as in Burma, where one general was ultimately simply replaced by another? Or would it have gone up in flames, like the governments of Ben Ali and Qaddafi?

We'll never know. But the chance of collapse wasn't zero. Such brittle systems often rest on one man's pulse, and Kim Jong-il was already ailing after his 2008 stroke. His heart might not have survived the strain—rumours say that his

2011 death followed an explosive fit of rage. Had he died amid an uprising, the state could have cracked. Kim Jong-un, still untested, might have lacked the clout to seize command. A general or a cadre—like Jong-un's ambitious uncle Jang Song-thaek, could have made a move. Should the regime have disintegrated, the peninsula might have raced towards reunification, ending the North's long nightmare.

16

The Final Stroke
Kim Jong-un could have suffered a fatal heart attack in 2020

After his stroke in 2008, Kim Jong-il was living on borrowed time. The Great Commander himself understood this, at least to some extent. The campaign to promote his son was unfolding far faster than the one Kim Jong-il had experienced under Kim Il-sung. He also set about revitalising the top Party institutions. In September 2010, a Party Conference was convened—the first major Party event since 1980—and the Politburo and Secretariat were refilled with new appointees. It was also here that Kim Jong-un was publicly introduced and commissioned as General of the Army, his formal rank finally matching his title as the Young General.

It appears Kim Jong-il planned to live at least until April 2012. That date would mark the 100th anniversary of Kim Il-sung's birth and there is good reason to believe that Kim Jong-il intended to promote himself to Generalissimo, mirroring his father's self-promotion in 1992. This would have signalled the Great Commander's preparations for semi-retirement, while his chosen successor readied to take the reins. Even the rank insignia had been prepared, waiting for the big day—a victor's wreath encircling a large star. Later, one could see them displayed near Kim Jong-il's coffin.

All plans were abruptly cut short by Kim's death in December 2011. In a twist, it was his own schemes that denied him the apotheosis. Born in 1941, in the 1970s he had altered his official birth year to 1942, to create a neat thirty-year gap with his father, who was born in 1912. Had he not done so, Kim could have celebrated his seventieth birthday in February 2011. Instead, the fabricated date forced him to wait until 2012—a year he never reached.

From what we know, the cause of death was surprisingly mundane—an outburst of anger. In December 2011, Kim received a report that a dam in Huichon, under construction since 2009 and visited by the Great Commander at least eight times, was riddled with flaws and leaks. Furious, Kim ordered immediate repairs and planned to visit the site the next day. But fate had other plans. On the morning of 17 December 2011, he was dead.

Despite the sudden and unexpected end to Kim Jong-il's life, the Kim family's rule remained unbroken. Initially, very few were informed—even the country's Prime Minister, Choe Yong-nim, was in the countryside, unaware of what had transpired.

The world only learned of Kim Jong-il's demise two days later, on 19 December, when Korean Central Television broadcast a special announcement at noon. The news shocked everyone, including South Korean President Lee Myung-bak, whose own (real) seventieth birthday was abruptly overshadowed by the emergency.

The announcement was clear: 'Today Comrade Kim Jong-un, the great successor of the great deed of the Juche revolution and the outstanding Leader of our Party, army and the people, stands at the head of our revolution.' This was also the last day Kim Jong-un's name crept onto Rodong Sinmun's pages in ordinary print; from the next edition, it blazed in bold, the typographic insignia of the Supreme Leader. Thus, a new era began.

Kim Jong-un was just 27 when he assumed power. Young and inexperienced, many speculated that the elite would turn him into a puppet. Yet Kim Jong-un quickly proved otherwise. Vice-Marshal Lee Yong-ho, empowered by Kim Jong-il as his de facto deputy on military affairs, was ousted in July 2012, vanishing from public view. Jang Song-thaek, Kim Jong-un's scheming uncle, was publicly purged in December 2013 amid accusations of disloyalty, degeneracy and corruption—accusations normally handled within the regime and not made public. The new master showed he was not afraid to wield the whip.

As I write in 2025, Kim Jong-un has been in power for over a decade. His rule has largely continued his father's legacy. The reformist momentum that began with the 2009 currency reform carried on until around 2015. Some developments in this period—such as decentralising state control over agriculture, industry and foreign trade between 2012 and 2014—did indeed help North Korea's economic growth. Optimistic analysts, perhaps blinded by wishful thinking, declared that 'Kim Jong-un is serious about reforms', hoping that he might become North Korea's Deng Xiaoping. But he never was. Like his predecessors, his primary focus remained preserving power.

His reign has seen a sharp decline in the number of escapees. The COVID-19 pandemic of the early 2020s aided this, as China shut its borders for years. Meanwhile, North Korea has made remarkable advances in weapons technology, proving that, while planned economies tend to be inefficient, specialised sectors—missiles, in this case—can develop at a blistering pace. Kim Jong-un's reckless diplomatic provocations of the mid-2010s drew heavy sanctions, after relentless nuclear and missile tests angered China. Yet his grip on power endured. The 2022 invasion of Ukraine by Vladimir Putin opened new avenues—North Korea began supplying munitions to Moscow in exchange for food, money and oil, and even dispatched a division-sized force to fight alongside the Russians.

It was almost a return to the blissful horror of the late Kim Il-sung era: a stable regime, economic mismanagement offset by foreign aid, and protection from foreign invasion—

once guaranteed by Moscow and Beijing, now secured by native nuclear bombs and intercontinental missiles.

There was only one moment when Kim Jong-un's grip on power seemed genuinely fragile. It came in April 2020, when the Supreme Leader—as he styled himself at the time—abruptly vanished from public view. His last known appearance was at a Politburo plenum, where the leadership had debated COVID strategy; elevated the Korean People's Army Chief of Staff, Pak Chong-chon, to full membership; and welcomed two new cadres: Foreign Minister Lee Son-gwon and Kim Jong-un's own sister, Kim Yo-jong, as alternate Politburo members.

Then, Kim Jong-un simply disappeared. The Supreme People's Assembly session convened the very next day went ahead without his august presence. That alone raised no immediate alarm; after all, the Supreme Leader had missed the previous session too, prompting whispers that he regarded the rubber-stamp legislature as a waste of time.

But there was one event he was unquestionably expected to attend. On 15 April, the Day of the Sun—Kim Il-sung's birthday—Kim Jong-un was meant to lead a solemn visit to pay homage at his grandfather's mausoleum, accompanied by the nation's top officials. Instead, *Rodong Sinmun* published photos of the elite gathered, saluting or bowing before the revered corpse, without Kim.

The international media erupted into speculation, some suggesting that Kim might have died. Remarkably, the online newspaper Daily NK's network again proved its mettle, revealing that the Supreme Leader was receiving cardiovascular treatment at the Hyangsan clinic. It was an unusual procedure for someone so young, but understandable, given the Kim family's genetic predisposition and Kim Jong-un's morbid obesity and smoking habits. The ominous setting added to the drama: after Kim Il-sung died of a heart attack in 1994, Kim Jong-il had ordered the demolition of the Myohyang villa where it had happened, and had a heart clinic built nearby, lamenting that such a facility in July 1994 might perhaps have prolonged the Great Leader's life. It seemed that history was repeating itself and the Myohyang mountains might claim another tyrant.

The crisis, however, was brief. When North Korean media published Kim Jong-un's letter to Syrian President Bashar al-Assad on 17 April, marking Syria's Independence Day, most concluded that Kim was indeed alive—no one in the elite would have dared to forge a message in his name. Still, rumours persisted. Ji Song-ho, a South Korean legislator of North Korean origin caught up in hopeful fantasy, insisted regime change was imminent, even asserting there was a '99%' chance that Kim was dead. He was soon proven wrong. On 1 May, Kim Jong-un made a public appearance at the opening ceremony of a fertiliser factory; once this was reported, the rumours swiftly died down.

Kim clearly learned from this episode. In the years that followed, he established the position of First Secretary of the Central Committee, effectively a deputy to the General Secretary, who could preside over meetings in his absence. While the role remains vacant, it grants Kim vital flexibility. In 2022, he introduced his daughter to the public, sparking speculation that he sees her as his potential heir. And from 2023 on, Kim started quietly loosening what had long looked like an ironclad rule: show up at the mausoleum, every time, without fail. The rituals not only burdened him—he had not been present when his father and grandfather constructed the cult of the family—but also risked exposing his health vulnerabilities. He did not act hastily—still young and with time on his side—but the experience appears to have landed as an unsettling glimpse of his own vulnerability and, ultimately, his mortality.

This, of course, leaves us with another tantalising counterfactual—what if he had died? What if the doctors hadn't reached him in time? Or if they had, but had failed?

The North Korean elite would have been caught utterly off-guard. Each previous time a Leader had passed, a successor had already been chosen. Never before had the regime been left without a path to follow. This time, there was no plan, no heir apparent—just silence and speculation.

Who would have succeeded Kim Jong-un? In 2020, the foreign press had one favourite: his sister, Kim Yo-jong. North Korea has always been ruled by the Kim family, the narrative went; so, naturally, the sister will be next. But this convenient logic didn't hold up under scrutiny. In North Korea, tradition is that a leader is succeeded by his son—always a son—and he is preordained long before the funeral wreaths are laid. Kim Yo-jong was neither son nor successor. She was a woman in a patriarchal state that hasn't seen a female monarch since the seventh-century queens of Silla—who ruled far to the south. More to the point, no one had named her. Her position—Deputy Chief of a department, alternate Politburo member—echoed not a successor-in-waiting, but the sidelined siblings of North Korean history: Kim Kyong-hui, Kim Jong-il's sister; Kim Yong-ju, Kim Il-sung's brother. Both were powerful. Both were passed over.

And then there was the unspoken truth: why hand over the throne to someone else when you might just seize it yourself? In the brutal hierarchy of Pyongyang, the safest place to be is at the top. Every official worth their salt recalled how, after Kim Jong-un's rise, the ambitious were rapidly culled by the new Supreme Leader.

So, if not Kim Yo-jong, then who? Perhaps the best candidate was not a blood relative at all, but a man from the elite's inner sanctum: Choe Ryong-hae. By 2020, Choe stood at the very summit of power, save for the Supreme Leader himself. He was one of just three men on the Politburo Presidium, alongside Kim and the ageing Pak Pong-ju, former reformist Prime Minister. Choe had recently been granted two lofty titles: Chairman of the Presidium of the Supreme People's Assembly and, more tellingly, First Deputy Chairman of the State Affairs Commission. The latter title is normally treated as ceremonial. But this time, the state press gave Choe a special paragraph, a gesture previously reserved only for chosen heirs. In the cryptic language of North Korean signalling, it felt like a scream.

Who is Choe Ryong-hae? His story begins, inevitably, with his father. Choe Hyon was one of Kim Il-sung's closest comrades during the anti-Japanese struggle. The famed Pochonbo raid was staged, in part, to rescue Choe Hyon's embattled unit. After independence, he rose to become Minister of the People's Armed Forces. Two persistent rumours hint at the man's extraordinary clout. One: Choe Hyon continued to call Kim Il-sung simply 'Il-sung', even as the rest of the country grovelled with titles like 'Great Leader'. Two: he played a key role in engineering Kim Jong-il's selection as heir in the 1970s.

His son, Choe Ryong-hae, was born in 1950, and began his own ascent in the Youth League during the 1980s. Then came disaster. In the late '90s, he was purged: restricted-access compromising material, released from the top, painted him as a grotesquely corrupt sadist. One such report claimed that Kim Jong-il himself was shocked by Choe's extravagant lifestyle. Another alleged that he forced women marked for labour camps to become his concubines, in exchange for clemency, and treated them with depravity. It was a sordid fall.

Yet, remarkably, Choe Junior clawed his way back. In 2003 he returned to office, taking over as Party boss in North Hamgyong Province. By 2010, he was awarded the rank of four-star general—alongside none other than Kim Jong-un. That same year, he became an alternate Politburo member, while Kim was merely a Central Committee member. Under Kim Jong-un, Choe's career became a game of snakes and ladders. He rocketed to Vice-Marshal in 2012 and joined the Politburo Presidium, skipping over the rank of full member. He looked absurd in uniform, pinned with a Kim Il-sung University badge instead of a military academy's. He had no military training. But in the Kims' North Korea, loyalty trumps skill.

Later, he was challenged by another high-flyer, Hwang Pyong-so. But Choe won that bout too, reportedly providing evidence of Hwang's corruption. In 2017, he seized control of the Organisation and Guidance Department—arguably the most powerful organ in the whole regime, overseeing personnel and purges alike. There were whispers that his family ties had also grown stronger: Kim Yo-jong's husband, they said—Kim Jong-un's brother-in-law—was none other than Choe Ryong-hae's son.

So what would it have meant if Kim Jong-un had died in 2020, and Choe had emerged to 'stand at the helm of our revolution'?

We cannot know. But we can guess.

It wouldn't have been entirely unthinkable for Chairman Choe to strike out in a new direction. Lavrentiy Beria—Stalin's own depraved fixer—turned out to be a closet reformer when his time came. Choe, with his reputation for cruelty and cunning, could well have seen reforms as his only hope for legitimacy in this scenario. In fact, it would have been a necessity. Breaking the Kim bloodline would break the spell. A new story would need to be written.

It was precisely to prevent such outcomes that Kim Il-sung enshrined dynastic succession. He understood something fundamental about power: it flows safest through the blood. And while North Korea has flirted with instability, and tiptoed along the edge of chaos more than once, the hereditary principle has held—fragile, absurd, yet strangely resilient.

It has held through famine, through repression and suffering, and even through dissent and rebellion. It holds still.

For now.

Conclusion
Future in the Past?

They say that history rarely offers second chances. They are wrong, of course. North Korea, it seems, has had at least sixteen. The country's story is often told as a tale of unbroken totalitarian control, an eternal dynasty standing above the never-ending suffering. But even that near-flawless system of despotic oppression has not been truly invincible.

Some of these moments came at birth: the 1940s and early 1950s were years of flux, when Soviet favour, American action or sheer luck made all the difference. These were the regime's most fragile days, when it hadn't yet wrapped itself in myth. The aftermath of Stalin's death, and Khrushchev's turn against cults of personality, saw Pyongyang wobble in the mid-1950s. Had Soviet or Chinese leaders pushed a little harder, had Kim Il-sung's rivals been a little smarter, the era of the Great Leader might have ended before it truly began.

Then came the years when collapse should have been inevitable: the 1990s, with their famine and economic ruin. The Soviet Union had vanished. China was reforming. Kim Il-sung was dead. But still, the regime survived. It survived not because it was strong, but because the world looked away; the elites hesitated; and the people, never given a chance for a change, endured in silence.

Other crises have come not from historical tides but from the missteps and mortality of those at the top. North Korea might have vanished in a puff of smoke had its leaders made one more blunder—launched one more war, mishandled one more reform, or failed to climb out of one more health scare. In a state where one man holds so much power, the whole system teeters on his heartbeat.

And yet, for all that, the regime has shown remarkable resilience—not because it is just or wise, but because it has become an ecosystem of fear, loyalty and self-preservation. The 1970s and '80s offered the Kims a long, terrible calm, and today, Kim Jong-un's rule seems similarly solid—at least from a distance. For the North Korean people, this is stability not as blessing, but as curse.

This book has examined sixteen moments—some dramatic, others obscure—when the course of North Korean history could have shifted, perhaps decisively. In some scenarios, the regime collapses in flames; in others, it crumbles from within. A few offer glimmers of gradual reform, or even peaceful reunification. None of these paths were taken, and yet, their very plausibility reminds us of a central truth: history, even in North Korea, is not carved in stone.

CONCLUSION

Today, North Korea appears immoveable. It has endured famines, sanctions, diplomatic isolation and internal upheavals, and still it survives. Since the mid-2000s, it has armed itself with nuclear weapons. Since 2020, it has locked its borders more tightly than ever before. Its leaders have made clear their determination to rule forever, and many outsiders—policymakers, journalists and even seasoned North Korea-watchers—have come to view the regime as permanent, unchangeable, impervious to internal or external pressure. Realpolitik, they argue, is the only approach: containment, deterrence, deals.

Such thinking, while practical in the short term, can become paralysing in the long run. It assumes that the future will mirror the past, and that the window for change has already closed. This book argues otherwise. Again and again, history has presented North Korea with choices—some of them visible in real time, others only apparent in hindsight. And, time and again, those choices have been shaped not by destiny, but by contingency, accident and the unpredictable decisions of fallible men.

There are important lessons in this. First, the regime's survival should not be confused with its legitimacy or security. It has endured not because of popular choice, but because it has crushed all alternatives. Second, the idea that change must come from outside—through pressure or negotiation—overlooks the long record of internal volatility and criticism. Even the most totalitarian systems contain the seeds of their own undoing. Often those seeds sprout in silence, invisible until it is too late.

Of course, none of this is a call for naïveté. One should not expect North Korea to collapse tomorrow, or believe that goodwill alone will thaw a regime built on cruelty and fear. But it would be equally misguided to assume that change is impossible, or that every future outcome must be negotiated across a table. One of the most striking insights from these sixteen crises is that pivotal turning points often emerge far from the public eye: a secret memo, a stroke of illness, a failed coup, a single decision made behind a closed door.

In that sense, the history of North Korea is not only a history of oppression—it is also a history of unrealised alternatives. To understand those alternatives is not to indulge in fantasy. It is to acknowledge that what is, could easily have been otherwise—and might still be. For all its frozen rituals and rigid hierarchy, North Korea remains, like any society, a dynamic entity. Its rulers may seek to control the future, but they cannot erase the past. And that past is full of narrow escapes, missed exits, and fragile branches that bent but did not break.

This book began as an exercise in counterfactual history. But it ends with a more modest hope: that, in remembering how often the fate of North Korea has hung in the balance, we remain open to the idea that it may do so again, and that things may end differently next time. Realpolitik is

CONCLUSION

necessary—but not sufficient. Beneath the concrete monuments and the endless parades, change remains possible.

This story is not over yet. North Korea remains a state of men, not gods. Their hearts can fail, their decisions can falter. More dangerously for them, the world is still changing. A political earthquake in Beijing, a breach of loyalty in the military or simply an ordinary North Korean deciding to say 'no'—these can still bring down the system.

To any North Korean who might one day read this: the future is not written. Your country's fate has come close to changing many times. It may yet do so. Regimes, like storms, can rage for decades, but they always pass. And when the sky clears, the land is still there, waiting to be rebuilt.

Index

Abe Nobuyuki, 32–4
Agreed Framework (1994), 128–9
Albania, 8, 82, 136–7
Alia, Ramiz, 136
American Samoa, 2
An Jong-ho, 118
Anami Korechika, 27
Arab Spring (2010–11), 169
Arnold, Archibald, 39
al-Assad, Bashar, 176
August Plenum (1956), 82–9, 91–9, 113, 167
Austria, 6, 31, 43–4, 45
Axis of Evil, 129

Ba'ath Party, 121
Belgian Congo (1908–60), 25
Ben Ali, Zine El Abidine, 169
Beneš, Edvard, 39
Beria, Lavrentiy, 52, 181
Berlin, Germany, 31, 44
Blue House raid (1968), 102–9
Blue Shirts Society, 60

Bonesteel III, Charles, 24
Bouazizi, Mohamed, 169
Brezhnev, Leonid, 108, 109
Bulgaria, 82, 123
Burma, 169
Bush, George Walker, 129, 154

Cambodia, 119, 122
Carter, James 'Jimmy', 128
Ceaușescu, Nicolae, 123
Chang Shi-u, 53
Cheng Xiaohe, 102
Chernenko, Konstantin, 115
Chervenkov, Valko, 82
Chiang Kai-shek, 29, 68
China, *see* People's Republic of China; Republic of China
Chinese Character Simplification Scheme (1956), 87
Chinese Civil War (1927–49), 29, 31, 42, 64, 68
Chinese Communist Party, 8, 29, 48, 80, 83

INDEX

Chinese Koreans, 80, 93
Chistyakov, Ivan, 35, 36–7, 50, 56
Cho Jae-guk, 60, 61
Cho Man-shik, 29, 53
Choe Chang-ik, 82–3, 85–9, 93–4, 167
Choe Gwang, 119
Choe Ha-yong, 32–4
Choe Hyon, 179
Choe Ki-song, 60
Choe Ryong-hae, 178–81
Choe Song, 180
Choe Yong-gon, 68, 82, 85
Choe Yong-nim, 172
Chon Byong-ho, 151, 152
Chongjin, North Korea, 139–44, 167
Chongno, 62
Chosen-jingu, Keijo, 34
Chosun Ilbo, 54
Chun Doo-hwan, 106
Chung Il-kwon, 105–6, 109
Churchill, Winston, 21, 22–3
Civil Rights Movement (1954–68), 78, 108
Clinton, William 'Bill', 127–31, 144
collectivisation, 87
Communist Party of Austria, 43
Communist Party of China, *see* Chinese Communist Party

Communist Party of Greece, 75–6
Communist Party of Korea, 35, 38, 39, 41, 45–6, 50, 53, 55–6, 63
Communist Party of the Soviet Union, 1, 9–10, 12, 82, 83, 92, 115
coup attempts in North Korea
    August Plenum (1956), 82–9, 91–9, 113, 167
    Frunze Academy plot (1992), 114–24, 152
    Sixth Corps' rebellion (1995), 139–44, 150, 158
COVID-19 pandemic, 15–16, 174, 175, 185
Cuba, 1, 2
cults of personality, 1, 6, 57, 82–9, 92, 135, 153
Cultural Revolution in China (1966–76), 87–9, 98
currency revaluation in North Korea (2009), 163–70, 174
Czechoslovakia (1918–92), 39, 98

Day of the Sun, 117, 137, 175
demilitarised zone (DMZ), 135
Democratic People's Republic of Korea (1948–), *see* North Korea
Deng Xiaoping, 116, 118, 174

INDEX

Dubček, Alexander, 98
Dubna, Russia, 125

East Germany (1949–90), 42–3, 123, 124
EC-121 shootdown (1969), 101
Egypt, 118
Eisenhower, Dwight, 77
Endo Ryusaku, 33, 34
Equatorial Guinea, 119, 122

famine in North Korea (1994–2000), 13, 139–44, 147, 158, 162, 183
France, 21, 156, 159
Frunze Academy, 116, 121, 123, 152

Gao Gang, 72
de Gaulle, Charles, 31
General Political Bureau, 152, 153
Geneva Agreement (1994), 128–9
Germany
    East Germany (1949–90), 42–3, 123, 124
    Nazi Germany (1933–45), 21, 24, 31, 43, 49, 60
    West Germany (1949–90), 42–3
Gorbachev, Mikhail, 12, 115–16, 118

Gottwald, Klement, 39
Great Leap Forward (1958–62), 87, 98
Greece, 75–6, 77
Grósz, Károly, 123

Hamhung, North Korea, 50, 54
Han Jong-suk, 149
Han Song-ryong, 151
Han Un-suk, 149
Hao Deqing, 102
Harrison, William, 21–2
Heavenly Way, 54
Hegay, Aleksei, 54, 55, 57, 81
Hiranuma Kiichiro, 26
Hirohito, Emperor of Japan, 26–7, 28
Hiroshima atomic bombing (1945), 23–8, 33
Hodge, John, 37
Hokkaido, Japan, 25
Hong Kye-song, 117, 118
Hoxha, Enver, 8, 136
Hu Jintao, 154
Huichon, North Korea, 172
Hun Sen, 122
Hungary, 82, 98, 123
Hussein, Saddam, 13, 121
Hwang Pyong-so, 180
hwanggup, 120
Hyangsan, North Korea, 176

Ignatyev, Aleksandr, 56

INDEX

Ihara Junjiro, 32
Imjin River, 103
Inchon, South Korea, 70
India, 72
industrialisation, 87
influenza, 166–7
International Atomic Energy Agency (IAEA), 127, 128
Internet, 2, 4
Iraq, 13, 121
Italy, 2
Ivanov, Vasiliy, 84, 86
Izvestiya, 40

Jang Song-thaek, 14, 151, 157, 170, 173
Japan, 3, 6, 8, 21–30, 31–5, 114, 117
    atomic bombings (1945), 23–8, 33
    colonial rule in Korea (1910–45), 23, 28, 32–5, 48, 60, 79, 109
    Operation Downfall plan (1945), 23
    Soviet War (1945), 21–4, 25, 26, 33–5, 47, 49
    surrender (1945), 6, 25–8, 32–5, 52, 53
    US occupation (1945–52), 28, 31
Ji Song-ho, 176
Jiang Zemin, 154
Jo Myong-rok, 152–4, 156

Johnson, Lyndon Baines, 108
Joint American–Soviet Commission (1945–7), 37–41, 56
Joint Declaration on Denuclearisation (1992), 127

Kang Kon Military Academy, 168
Kang Sok-chu, 150
Kang Yong-hwan, 117
Kayama Kaei, *see* Choe Ha-yong
Keijo, Korea, *see* Seoul, South Korea
Khabarovsk, Russia, 6, 49
Khrushchev, Nikita, 86, 89, 94–9, 136
    secret speech (1956), 1, 2, 9–10, 12, 75, 82, 83, 92, 94, 153, 183
Kim Chaek, 54
Kim Chan, 54, 55
Kim Du-bong, 53
Kim Gwang-jin, 53
Kim Hyong-jip, 60, 61–2
Kim Il-chol, 152
Kim Il-hun, 118
Kim Il-sung, 6–12, 30, 37, 39, 40, 46, 47–58, 59–64, 174
    assassination attempt (1946), 40–41, 59–64

INDEX

August Plenum (1956),
    82–9, 91–9, 113, 167
birthday, 117, 137, 175
Blue House raid (1968),
    102–9
CCP membership (1931–
    45), 8, 48
Choe Hyon, relationship
    with, 179
collectivisation, 87
cult of personality, 6, 57,
    82–9, 92, 135, 153
death (1994), 12, 13,
    133–7, 139, 176, 183
Frunze Academy plot
    (1992), 114–24, 152
Group for People's Welfare,
    involvement in, 89, 94
historical revisionism, 114,
    117, 119–20
industrialisation, 87
Khrushchev's secret speech
    (1956), 9–10, 12, 82,
    83, 92
Korean War (1950–53), 9,
    11, 42, 47, 57, 58, 64,
    67–78, 93, 95, 97
leadership appointment
    (1945), 47–58
mausoleum, 13, 133, 175
Non-Proliferation Treaty
    accession (1985), 126–7
nuclear programme,
    125–8

purges (1950s), 81–2, 85–6,
    93, 94, 95
Separate Infantry Brigade
    service (1942–5), 49,
    54, 80
Singular Thought System
    (1967), 11, 113
Sino-Soviet split (1960–
    89), 10, 86–7, 97
Soviet Union, life in
    (1940–45), 49
succession, 12, 97, 114–15,
    133–7, 139, 171
Kim Il-sung University, 180
Kim Jong-chol, 151, 157
Kim Jong-il, 12–14, 97, 114,
    171–3
    birthday, 171–2
    China visits, 148
    cinephilia, 13
    cult of personality, 153
    currency revaluation
        (2009), 163–70, 174
    death (2011), 159, 170,
        171–3
    famine (1994–2000), 13,
        139–44, 147, 158, 162,
        183
    father's death (1994),
        133–7
    Frunze Academy plot
        (1992), 114–24, 152
    horse riding accident
        (1993), 156

nuclear programme, 13, 128–9
Ryongchon disaster (2004), 148–54, 157–8, 162
Sixth Corps' rebellion (1995), 139–44, 150, 158
stroke (2008), 155–9, 169, 171
Sun Train, 148–54
womanising, 13, 115
Kim Jong-nam, 150, 157
Kim Jong-ui, 60, 61
Kim Jong-un, 14–16, 151, 159, 161, 170, 173
border sealing (2020), 15–16, 174, 185
nuclear programme, 15, 174, 175
stroke (2020), 15, 175–81
successor designation (2009), 159, 161, 171
Kim Kyong-hui, 157, 178
Kim Phyong-il, 115
Kim Shin-jo, 104–5
Kim Yo-jong, 175, 177–8, 180
Kim Yong-bom, 53, 55
Kim Yong-chun, 141, 142–3, 150, 152, 157–8
Kim Yong-il, 115
Kim Yong-ju, 152, 178
Kim Yong-nam, 119, 151–2
Kim Young-sam, 129–30, 144
Kissinger, Henry, 126
Ko Yong-hui, 134

Korea
Democratic People's Republic (DPRK) (1948–), *see* North Korea
Japanese colony (1910–45), 23, 28, 32–5, 48, 60, 79, 109
Republic of Korea (1948–), *see* South Korea
reunification prospects, 6, 9, 43, 123–4
Soviet occupation (1945–8), 21–30, 31–2, 35–42, 59, 67
US occupation (1945–8), 24–5, 31–2, 35–42, 67
Korean Central Television, 173
Korean language, 88
Korean People's Army
Blue House raid (1968), 102–9
Frunze Academy plot (1992), 114–24, 152
Kim Il-sung death announcement (1986), 135
NPT withdrawal crisis (1993), 127–31
Sixth Corps' rebellion (1995), 139–44, 150, 158
Korean People's Revolutionary Army, 114, 117, 119–20

INDEX

Korean script, 88
Korean War (1950–53), 9, 11, 42, 47, 57, 58, 64, 67–78, 167
   bioweapons allegations, 97
   China and, 9, 42, 68, 69, 70–75, 93, 95, 125
   nuclear weapons and, 125
   Soviet Union and, 9, 42, 47, 57, 58, 64, 67–75
   United States and, 9, 11, 42, 70–71, 77, 78, 97, 125
Korotkov List, 51, 55
Kozuki Yoshio, 35, 36, 45
Krenz, Egon, 123
Krishtul, Boris, 52
Kuril Islands, 31
Kye Ung-thae, 119, 151, 156

labour camps, 4, 86, 114, 124, 142, 179–80
Laos, 1, 119, 122
Lebedev, Nikolay, 40, 51–2, 56, 58
Lee Hui-du, 60
Lee Je-gang, 159
Lee Jong-ok, 119
Lee Sang-jo, 83, 85, 91–3
Lee Son-gwon, 175
Lee Song-ryol, 60, 61
Lee Sung-yop, 68, 70, 74, 81
Lee Yong-ho, 173
Lee Yong-mu, 152

Libya, 169
Lin Biao, 12, 114
Loboda, Ivan, 54

MacArthur, Douglas, 36–7, 71, 77, 125
Manchuria, 29, 48, 72, 76, 80, 94, 120
Manhattan Project (1942–6), 23–4, 25–8
Manila, Philippines, 21
Mansu Hill, Pyongyang, 137
Mansudae Grand Monument, Pyongyang, 137
Mao Zedong
   Albania, relations with, 136
   August Plenum incident (1956), 83, 85, 93, 95
   Cultural Revolution (1966–76), 87–9, 98
   Great Leap Forward (1958–62), 87, 98
   Lin Biao appointment (1969), 12, 114
   PRC founding (1949), 29, 42, 64, 68
   Sino-Soviet split (1960–89), 10, 86–7, 97
Marxism, 8–9
May Day, 55–6
Mikoyan, Anastas, 91, 93–4, 95, 97
missile technology, 174–5

INDEX

Mladenov, Petar, 123
Mongolia, 83, 114, 134
Moscow Decision (1945), 37–8, 39
Mun Il, 50, 54, 68, 73, 80–81
My Journey at the Nuclear Brink (Perry), 127, 129
Myohyang mountains, 133–4, 176

Nagasaki atomic bombing (1945), 23–4, 25, 26, 33
Nagasaki Yuzo, 34
Nagy, Imre, 98
Nakajima Ikken, 109
Nam Il, 80
National Defence Commission, 135, 152–3, 156, 157, 158
National Geographic, 24
Nazi Germany (1933–45), 21, 24, 31, 43, 49, 60
Ne Win, 169
Nixon, Richard, 126
Non-Proliferation Treaty (1968), 126–31
Norodom Sihanouk, King of Cambodia, 119, 122
North Korea
  August Plenum (1956), 82–9, 91–9, 113, 167
  border, 15–16, 85, 147, 174, 185
  collectivisation, 87
  constitution (1948), 41, 69
  COVID-19 pandemic, 15–16, 174, 175, 185
  currency revaluation (2009), 163–70, 174
  EC-121 shootdown (1969), 101
  famine (1994–2000), 13, 139–44, 147, 158, 162, 183
  founding of (1948), 41
  Frunze Academy coup plot (1992), 114–24, 152
  historical revisionism, 114, 117, 119–20
  industrialisation, 87
  influenza epidemic (2009–10), 166–7
  Joint Declaration on Denuclearisation (1992), 127
  Kim Il-sung's death (1994), 12, 13, 133–7, 139, 176, 183
  Kim Jong-il's death (2011), 159, 170, 171–3
  Korean War (1950–53), 9, 11, 42, 47, 57, 58, 64, 67–78, 93, 95, 97
  labour in, 4, 114
  Non-Proliferation Treaty and, 126–31
  nuclear programme, 13,

INDEX

15, 124, 125–31, 153–4, 174–5, 185
prison camps, 4, 86, 114, 124, 142, 179–80
Pueblo incident (1968), 101
Ryongchon disaster (2004), 148–54, 157–8, 162
Singular Thought System (1967), 11, 113
Sixth Corps' rebellion (1995), 139–44, 150, 158
state price adjustment (2002–3), 162
North Vietnam (1945–76), 101, 107–8
Novichenko, Yakov, 61
Nozoe Masanori, 48
nuclear programme of North Korea, 13, 15, 124, 125–31, 153–4, 174–5, 185
  Agreed Framework (1994), 128–9
  Non-Proliferation Treaty, 126–31
Nyongbyon Nuclear Research Centre, 126, 127, 129, 130

O Jin-u, 119, 135–6
O Kuk-ryol, 152
Obiang Nguema Mbasogo, Teodoro, 119, 122
Okinawa, Japan, 35
Ongjin Peninsula, 67–8
Operation Downfall plan (1945), 23
OpPlan 5027, 130

Paek Se-bong, 152
Pak Chang-ok, 81–2, 87, 96–7
Pak Chong-ae, 53, 55–6, 57
Pak Chong-chon, 175
Pak Chong-ho, 53
Pak Hon-yong, 39, 40, 53, 58, 63–4, 67, 68, 72, 81, 83
Pak Il-san, 97
Pak Ir-u, 72, 74, 81
Pak Ki-so, 120
Pak Nam-gi, 162, 163, 167
Pak Pong-ju, 150, 151, 161–2, 178
Pak Pyong-nyul, 54, 55
Pak Sok-yun, 33–4
Pak Song-chol, 119, 152
Pak Ui-wan, 87, 96, 97–8
Pang Hak-se, 80
Papagos, Alexandros, 77
Park Chung-hee, 102–9
Peng Dehuai, 73, 91, 93, 95–6
People's Republic of China (1949–), 1, 2, 86, 136, 154, 183
  August Plenum (1956), 85–9, 91–9, 113
  Chinese Character Simplification Scheme (1956), 87
  Chongjin consulate, 143

INDEX

COVID-19 pandemic (2019–23), 174
Cultural Revolution (1966–76), 87–9, 98
foundation (1949), 29, 42, 64, 68
Great Leap Forward (1958–62), 87, 98
Kim Jong-il's visits, 148
Korean War (1950–53), 9, 42, 68, 69, 70–75, 93, 95, 125
Lin Biao appointment (1969), 12, 114
Nixon's visit (1972), 126
North Korean border, 15–16, 85, 147, 174, 185
reform and opening (1978–), 1, 2, 116, 118, 147, 174
Sino-Soviet split (1960–89), 10, 86–7, 97
Tiananmen massacre (1989), 134
People's Republic of Korea (1945–6), 35–6, 45
perestroika (1985–91), 12, 115–16, 117, 118
Perry, William, 127, 129
Philippines, 21
Phomvihane, Kaysone, 119, 122
Phyongsong, North Korea, 167

Poland, 2
Pravda, 37, 40, 62
Provisional People's Committee of North Korea, 59
Pueblo, USS, 101
Putin, Vladimir, 174
Putivets, Aleksandr, 143
Pyongyang, North Korea, 44, 50, 53, 56
  Chinese Koreans in, 93
  currency revaluation (2009), 165–6, 174
  dialect, 88
  Frunze Academy plot (1992), (1992), 114–24, 152
  Kang Kon Military Academy, 168
  Kim Il-sung assassination attempt (1946), 40–41, 59–64
  Mansudae Grand Monument, 137
Pyongyang Defence Command, 118–24
Pyongyang Shinmun, 61

Qaddafi, Muammar, 169

Rákosi, Mátyás, 82
Razuvayev, Vladimir, 57
Red Army, 49, 54, 80
Renner, Karl, 43

INDEX

Republic of China (1912–)
  Blue Shirts Society, 60
  Civil War (1927–49), 29, 31, 42, 64, 68
  Japanese War (1937–45), 29, 32
  Korea occupation negotiations (1945), 22, 38, 45
  Manchuria campaign (1945), 29
  Tehran Conference (1943), 22
Republic of Korea (1948–), *see* South Korea
Rhee Syngman, 35, 40, 42, 45, 69, 71, 74–5
Rodman, Dennis, 14
Rodong Sinmun, 133, 158, 173, 175
Roh Tae-woo, 123–4
Romanenko, Andrei, 56
Romania, 123
Roosevelt, Franklin, 21–3
Roschin, Nikolai, 72
Roux, François-Xavier, 156, 159
Rusk, Dean, 24
Russian Federation (1991–), 143, 174
Ryongchon disaster (2004), 148–54, 157–8, 162

Sadat, Anwar, 118

Sakhalin, 31
Second World War (1939–45), 3, 5–6, 21–30, 31–5, 49
  atomic bombings (1945), 23–8, 33
  Japanese surrender (1945), 6, 25–8, 32–5, 52, 53
  Operation Downfall plan (1945), 23
  revisionist history, 114, 117, 119–20
  Soviet–Japanese War (1945), 21–4, 25, 26, 33–5, 47, 49
Seoul, South Korea, 24, 28, 32, 34–5, 44, 50, 53, 129–30, 131
  Korean War (1950–53), 69–70, 71
Separate Infantry Brigade, 88th, 49, 54, 80
Shabshin, Anatoliy, 63
Shabshina, Fanya, 63
Shang Yue, 48
Shinto, 34
Shtykov, Terentiy, 39, 42, 56, 57, 62–3, 67
Sigurimi, 136
Silla (57 BCE–CE 935), 178
Singular Thought System (1967), 11, 113
Sino-Soviet split (1960–89), 10, 86–7, 97

INDEX

Sinuiju, North Korea, 148, 154, 162, 166
Siphandone, Khamtai, 122
Sixth Corps' rebellion (1995), 139–44, 150, 158
So Hwi, 85
Sokcho, South Korea, 74
South Korea, 4, 11, 29
    Blue House raid (1968), 102–9
    founding of (1948), 41
    Joint Declaration on Denuclearisation (1992), 127
    Korean War (1950–53), 9, 11, 42, 47, 57, 58, 64, 67–78, 93, 95
    legislative election (1967), 106
    nuclear programme, 126
South Pyongan Provincial People's Committee, 60
Soviet Koreans, 54, 79–80, 81, 87
Soviet Union (1922–91), 1, 3, 5–6, 8, 9, 183
    August Plenum incident (1956), 82–9, 91–9, 113
    Austria occupation (1945–55), 43–4
    collapse (1989–91), 115, 127, 134, 183
    German invasion of (1941), 49
    Great Purge (1936–8), 30
    Japanese War (1945), 21–4, 25, 26, 33–5, 47, 49
    Joint American–Soviet Commission (1945–7), 37–41, 56
    Khrushchev's secret speech (1956), 1, 2, 9–10, 12, 75, 82, 83, 92, 94, 153, 183
    Kim Il-sung's installation (1945), 47–58, 79
    Korea occupation (1945–8), 21–30, 31–2, 35–42, 67
    Korean War (1950–53), 9, 42, 47, 57, 58, 64, 67–75, 125
    Non-Proliferation Treaty (1968), 126
    perestroika (1985–91), 12, 115–16, 117, 118
    Sino-Soviet split (1960–89), 10, 86–7, 97
    Soviet Koreans deportation (1937), 79–80
    Stalin's death (1953), 9, 12, 58, 73, 82, 157, 183
    Tehran Conference (1943), 22
    Yalta Conference (1945), 22–3
    Zachariadis' exile in (1949–73), 75–6

INDEX

Stalin, Joseph, 1, 2, 5–6, 8, 9, 12, 21–30, 84, 136
   Austrian State Treaty (1955), 44
   cult of personality, 9–10, 12, 75, 82, 83, 84, 92, 183
   death (1953), 9, 12, 58, 73, 82, 157, 183
   Great Purge (1936–8), 30
   Kim's installation (1945), 47–58, 79
   Korea occupation (1945–8), 21–30, 31–2, 35–42
   Korean War (1950–53), 9, 42, 47, 58, 64, 67–8, 71, 72, 73
   Yalta Conference (1945), 21–3
Stalin, Vasiliy, 157
Sun Train, 148–54
Sunam Market, Chongjin, 167
Sunchon, North Korea, 166
surveillance, 3, 7
Suzdalev, Sergei, 57
Suzuki Kantaro, 27
Syria, 169, 176

Taiwan, 31, 33
Takeshita Yoshiharu, 56
Tehran Conference (1943), 22
Tet Offensive (1968), 107–8
38th parallel, 24, 31–2, 67–8

Tiananmen massacre (1989), 134
Tito, Josip Broz, 136
Togo Shigenori, 26, 27
Toyoda Soemu, 27
Treaty on the Non-Proliferation of Nuclear Weapons (1968), 126–31
Truman, Harry, 24–5, 32, 42
Tula, Russia, 51
Tunisia, 169
Tunkin, Grigoriy, 57

Ukraine, 174
Umezu Yoshijiro, 27
United Kingdom, 21, 22–3, 27, 45
United Nations, 41, 70–71
United States of America
   Agreed Framework (1994), 128–9
   Austria occupation (1945–55), 43–4
   Bush administration (2001–9), 128, 154
   Civil Rights Movement (1954–68), 78, 108
   Clinton administration (1993–2001), 127–31, 144
   EC 121 shootdown (1969), 101
   Japan occupation (1945–52), 28, 31

INDEX

Jo Myong-rok's visit (2000), 153
Joint American–Soviet Commission (1945–7), 37–41, 56
Korea occupation (1945–8), 24–5, 31–2, 35–42, 67
Korean War (1950–53), 9, 11, 42, 70–71, 77, 78, 97
Manhattan Project (1942–6), 23–4, 25–8
Nixon administration (1969–74), 78, 126
Non-Proliferation Treaty (1968), 126
NPT withdrawal crisis (1993), 127–31
Pacific War (1941–5), 21–4
Pueblo incident (1968), 101, 107
Tehran Conference (1943), 22
Vietnam War (1955–75), 101, 107–8
Yalta Conference (1945), 21–3
Vienna, Austria, 31, 44
Vietnam, 1, 101, 107–8

Warsaw Pact, 115

Washington, George, 48
West Germany (1949–90), 42–3
White Shirts Society, 40–41, 59–64
Won Ung-hui, 120, 121

Yalta Conference (1945), 21–3
Yang Bin, 162
Yang Yong-sun, 53, 57, 58
Yemen, 169
Yo Un-hyong, 34, 35, 39, 40, 45–6
Yon Hyong-muk, 119, 150, 152, 156
Yonai Mitsumasa, 27
Yongbyon Nuclear Research Centre, 126, 127, 129, 130
Youth League, 179
Yu Song-chol, 54, 55
Yugoslavia (1918–92), 2, 129, 136
Yun Kong-hum, 85, 86
Yun Po-son, 106

Zachariadis, Nikos, 75–6
Zhang Yuanwei, 143
Zhou Baozhong, 49
Zhou Enlai, 73